Science 4 Today

Grade 4

by
Margaret Fetty

Frank Schaffer Publications®

Author: Margaret Fetty
Editor: Nathan Hemmelgarn

Frank Schaffer Publications®

Send all inquiries to:
Frank Schaffer Publications
8720 Orion Place
Columbus, Ohio 43240-2111

Science 4 Today—grade 4

ISBN: 0-7682-3524-3

2 3 4 5 6 7 8 9 10 POH 12 11 10 09 08

Table of Contents

Science and Technology

Science in Personal and Social Perspectives

History and the Nature of Science

What Is Science 4 Today?

Science 4 Today is a comprehensive yet quick and easy-to-use supplement designed to complement any science curriculum. Based on the National Science Education Standards (NSES), forty topics cover essential concepts that fourth-grade students should understand and know in natural science. During the course of four days, presumably Monday through Thursday, students complete questions and activities focusing on each topic in about ten minutes. On the fifth day, students complete a twenty-minute assessment to practice test-taking skills, including multiple choice, true-false, and short answer.

How Does It work?

Unlike many science programs, *Science 4 Today* adopts the eight major standards outlined by the NSES to ascertain students' science skills. The standards are:

- unifying concepts and processes in science.
- science as inquiry.
- physical science.
- life science.
- Earth and space science.
- science and technology.
- science in personal and social perspectives.
- history and nature of science.

The book supplies forty topics commonly found in the fourth-grade science curriculum. Educators can choose a topic confident that it will support their unit of study and at least one of the eight standards. The Skills and Concepts chart on pages 8–10 identifies the main concepts for each week to insure that the content aligns with the classroom topic. The Scope and Sequence chart further supports identifying the specific skills following the standards. The answer key, found on pages 93–112, is provided for both daily activities and general assessments.

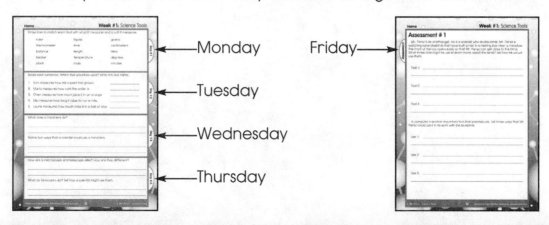

Monday

Tuesday

Wednesday

Thursday

Friday

How Was It Developed?

Science 4 Today was created in response to a need to assess students' understanding of important science concepts. Basals teach the necessary skills, but might not apply them to other overarching standards outlined by the NSES. Moreover, with the increased emphasis on standardized testing, the necessity for experience with test styles and semantics also becomes apparent.

How Can It Be Used?

Science 4 Today can be easily implemented into the daily routine of the classroom, depending on your teaching style. The activities and questions can be written on the board each day, or the whole page can be copied on a transparency and displayed at the appropriate time. It is also possible to copy the weekly page as a blackline master and distribute it at the beginning of each week. Students can complete the activities during attendance or other designated time. After completion, the class can briefly check and discuss the assignment.

What Are the Benefits?

The daily approach of *Science 4 Today* provides reading comprehension practice in science, higher-level thinking exercises, and problem-solving strategies. The pages also target test-taking skills by incorporating the style and syntax of standardized tests. Because of its consistent format, *Science 4 Today* not only offers opportunities for instruction but also serves as an excellent diagnostic tool.

Test-Taking Tips

Short Answer Questions

- Read the directions carefully. Be sure you know what you are expected to do. Ask questions if you do not understand.

- Read the whole question before you answer it. Some questions might have multiple parts.

- If you do not know the answer right away, come back to it after completing the other items.

- Review each question and answer after completing the whole test. Does your answer make sense? Does it answer the whole question?

- Check for spelling, punctuation, and grammar mistakes.

Multiple Choice Questions

- Read the question before looking at the answers. Then, come up with the answer in your head before looking at the choices to avoid confusion.

- Read all the answers before choosing the best answer.

- Eliminate answers that you know are not correct.

- Fill in the whole circle. Do not mark outside the circle.

- Review the questions and your answers after completing the whole test. Your first response is usually correct unless you did not read the question correctly.

True – False Questions

- Read each statement carefully. Look at the key words to understand the statement.

- Look at the qualifying words. Words like *all*, *always*, and *never* often signal a false statement. General words, like *sometimes*, *often*, and *usually*, most likely signal a true statement.

- If any part of the statement is false, the whole statement is false.

Skills and Concepts

Published by Frank Schaffer Publications. Copyright protected. 0-7682-3524-3 *Science 4 Today*

Week 28 - Pages 67 and 68
Robot Technology
robot
computer system
sensor
Mars rovers

Science in Personal and Social Perspectives
Week 29 - Pages 69 and 70
Body Systems
cell
tissue
organ
circulatory system
respiratory system
digestive system

Week 30 - Pages 71 and 72
Healthy Habits
food groups
exercise
nutrition label
hygiene

Week 31 - Pages 73 and 74
Pollution
land pollution
noise pollution
air pollution
water pollution
light pollution

Week 32 - Pages 75 and 76
Global warming
global warming
green house effect
balance of nature

Week 33 - Pages 77 and 78
Resources
natural resource
renewable resource
nonrenewable resource
inexhaustible resource
conserve

Week 34 - Pages 79 and 80
Changing Populations
population
environment
community

habitat

History and the Nature of Science
Week 35 - Pages 81 and 82
Conservation
extinct
endangered
protect
refuge
rain forest

Week 36 - Pages 83 and 84
Roman Contributions
central heat
aqueducts
sewage system
concrete
roads

Week 37 - Pages 85 and 86
Chinese Contributions
paper
printing
compass
gunpowder

Week 38 - Pages 87 and 88
The History of Flight
hot air balloons
airplanes
helicopter
rockets

Week 39 - Pages 89 and 90
Cycles in Nature
germinating seed
water cycle
seasons
life cycles

Week 40 - Pages 91 and 92
Child Inventors
Brandon Whale
Spencer Whale
Taylor Hernandez
inventions

Scope and Sequence

Skills/Concepts	1	2	3	4	5	6	7	8	9	10	11	12	13	14	15	16	17	18	19	20	21	22	23	24	25	26	27	28	29	30	31	32	33	34	35	36	37	38	39	40
Unifying Concepts and Processes in Science																																								
Systems		•						•	•	•		•	•				•				•							•							•	•				
Order and organization			•						•			•	•			•		•		•								•												
Measuring	•	•				•																																		
Science as Inquiry																																								
Science tools	•		•																				•																	
Science process skills					•					•																												•		
Scientific method				•																																		•		
Science inquiry					•					•																											•			•
Physical Science																																								
Properties of matter						•																																		
Force and motion							•			•														•	•											•				
Machines and their uses								•																				•												
Properties of electricity									•	•															•		•													
Properties of magnets										•															•	•											•			•
Properties of sound											•																													
Life Science																																								
Plant structures and functions												•																												
Animal classes													•																											
Heredity and diversity														•																										
Animal behaviors															•																								•	
Organisms and energy																•																								
Ecosystems																	•									•								•	•					
Earth and Space Science																																								
Moon																		•																						

• Indicates Skill or Concept Included

Scope and Sequence

Skills/Concepts	1	2	3	4	5	6	7	8	9	10	11	12	13	14	15	16	17	18	19	20	21	22	23	24	25	26	27	28	29	30	31	32	33	34	35	36	37	38	39	40
Earth's structure																			•		•	•				•														
Earth's materials																•				•													•			•				
Ocean																		•			•					•														
Natural disasters																						•																		
Weather																							•																	
Science and Technology																																								
Large human-made objects																								•												•				
Transportation																									•															
Ocean technology																										•														
Communication technology																											•													
Robot technology																												•												
Science in Personal and Social Perspectives																																								
Body systems																													•											
Healthy habits																														•						•				
Pollution																															•									
Global warming																																•								
Resources																																	•			•				
Populations																																		•						
History and Nature of Science																																								
Conservation																																			•					
Roman contributions																																				•				
Chinese contributions																																					•			
Flight																																						•		
Natural cycles																		•			•																		•	
Child inventors																																								•

• Indicates Skill or Concept Included

Write the name of a science tool to correctly complete each sentence.

1. Tia measures the length on an insect with a _____.

2. Carl uses a _____ to see if the water is hot enough.

3. Kim finds the mass of a rock using a _____.

4. Lana uses a _____ to measure six milliliters of water.

5. TJ watches the minute and second hands on the _____ to find out how long it takes the ice cube to melt.

What does a hand lens do?

_____

_____

Name two ways for a scientist to use a hand lens.

_____

_____

Explain how to use a balance to find mass.

_____

_____

_____

_____

_____

Tell what each tool does. Give an example of how you would use them.

microscope: _____

_____

telescope: _____

_____

binoculars:_____

_____

Assessment # 1

Fill in the circle next to the best answer.

1. What does a spring scale measure?

   (A) volume   (C) force

   (B) mass   (D) length

2. Which units are on a ruler?

   (A) degrees   (C) minutes

   (B) grams   (D) centimeters

Answer the questions.

3. Why would a scientist use a camera?

   _____

   _____

   _____

4. Why is the computer an important tool? Tell three ways that a scientist could use it.

   _____

   _____

   _____

   _____

   _____

   _____

   _____

   _____

What is the customary system of measurement?

_____

_____

_____

What is the metric system of measurement?

_____

Day #1

What measurement system is used in the science community?

_____

Why do all scientists use this system?

_____

_____

_____

Day #2

Write the abbreviation for each metric measurement word.

1. liter _____   4. centimeter _____   7. millimeter _____

2. gram _____   5. milliliter _____   8. decigram _____

3. meter _____   6. kilogram _____   9. kilometer_____

Day #3

Convert the measurements to make each equation true.

1. I L = _____ mL   5. 100 cL = _____ mL

2. I g = _____ cg   6. 0.I m = _____ cm

3. I m = _____ mm   7. 10 cg = _____ mg

4. 10 mg = _____ g   8. 10 L = _____ cL

Day #4

Assessment

Assessment # 2

Fill in the circle next to the best answer.

1. About what temperature is a popsicle?

   (A) –5°C   (C) 20°C

   (B) 10°C   (D) 32°C

2. About how long is a bee?

   (A) 2 m   (C) 2 mm

   (B) 2 cm   (D) 2 km

Write the name of an object that is about the size of each measurement.

3. 8 centimeters   _____

4. 1 meter   _____

5. 1 liter   _____

6. 100 milliliters _____

7. 1 gram   _____

Answer the question.

8. Antone jumped 9 meters, and Wes jumped 1,000 centimeters. Who jumped farther? Explain.

   _____

   _____

   _____

   _____

   _____

   _____

Draw a line to match each science process skill with its definition.

observing	grouping objects based on characteristics or qualities
classifying	using your five senses to learn about the world
communicating	telling how objects are alike and different
inferring	using what you know to make a guess about what will happen
predicting	sharing information using words, charts, diagrams, and graphs
comparing	using what you know and what you learn to make conclusions

Give an example of how you could use each science process skill.

making and using models: _____

_____

making operational definitions: _____

_____

What is a variable?

_____

Why would a scientist need to identify and control variables in an experiment?

_____

_____

_____

Name two reasons that scientists make measurements.

_____

_____

_____

_____

Assessment

Assessment # 3

Answer the questions.

1. Mia was doing an experiment about recycled wastes. For four weeks, she gathered data showing the materials that her family put in the recycling bin. The chart below shows her data. Use the information to make a graph beside the chart.

Material	Number of Pieces
aluminum	8
tin	2
plastics	3
glass	2
paper	5

2. At the end of four weeks, Mia made this graph. Write two conclusions that she can make.

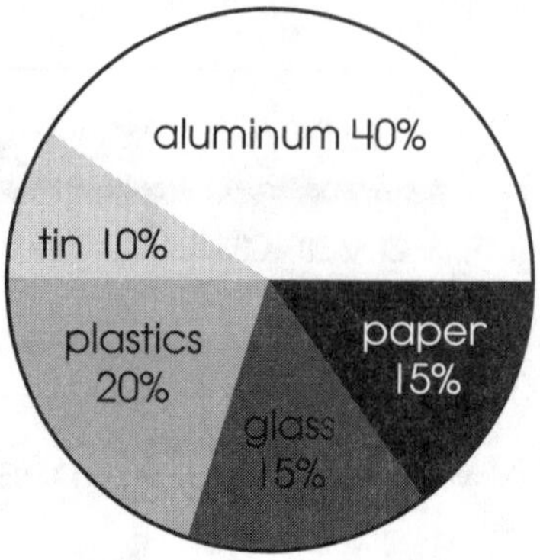

_____

_____

_____

_____

_____

_____

Fill in the circle next to the best answer.

3. Which science process skill did Mia use when she counted the recyclables?

(A) classifying   (C) inferring

(B) predicting   (D) estimating

4. Which science process skill did Mia use when she drew the graph?

(A) experimenting   (C) observing

(B) modeling   (D) communicating

Write numbers **1** through **8** to show the steps of the scientific method.

_____ Draw conclusions about the data

_____ Compare the conclusion with the hypothesis

_____ Plan the experiment and the variables

_____ State the problem

_____ Conduct the experiment

_____ Collect the data

_____ Communicate the results

_____ Make a hypothesis

What is a hypothesis?

_____

Circle the best hypothesis.

Does orange juice have more vitamins than apple juice?

Orange juice has more vitamin C than apple juice.

Orange juice tastes better than apple juice.

Jim is doing an experiment to find out what kind of materials will make a good bike reflector. What are three variables he might choose?

_____

_____

_____

In the experiment, how many variables will Jim change each time? Explain.

_____

_____

Write *true* or *false*.

1. _____ The problem is always stated as a question.

2. _____ The experiment's conclusion and hypothesis are always the same.

3. _____ The hypothesis is the final answer in an experiment.

4. _____ Scientists do not like to share the results of their experiments.

5. _____ When scientists interpret the data, they decide what the information means.

Assessment

Assessment # 4

Answer the questions.

1. Name two reasons why scientists follow the scientific method.

    _____

    _____

    _____

2. What will a scientist do if the hypothesis and conclusion do not match?

    _____

    _____

3. Why do scientists communicate information about their experiments?

    _____

    _____

Fill in the circle next to the best answer.

4. Which of the activities will a scientist not do during an experiment?

    (A) follow a set of steps

    (B) observe the action

    (C) change one variable

    (D) explain the action

5. Which step follows interpreting the data in the scientific method?

    (A) draw conclusions about the data

    (B) make a hypothesis

    (C) plan the experiment

    (D) state the problem

Scientists have certain characteristics that help them do their best work. Write **C** in front of each characteristic that you think is important for a scientist to have.

_____ curious   _____ patient   _____ creative

_____ watchful   _____ speedy   _____ uninterested

_____ careless   _____ eager   _____ persistent

Choose two characteristics. Tell why they are important qualities for a scientist to have.

_____

_____

Communication is another important characteristic in a scientist. Name three ways that a scientist might communicate.

_____

_____

_____

_____

Think about your characteristics. Would you make a good scientist? Explain. Give two examples to support your opinion.

_____

_____

_____

_____

_____

Draw a line to match each kind of scientist with the area the person studies.

botanist   someone who studies organisms and their environment

zoologist   someone who studies outer space

astronomer   someone who studies plants

physicist   someone who studies the matter, especially atoms and molecules

chemist   someone who studies matter and energy and their reactions

ecologist   someone who studies animals

Assessment # 5

Assessment

Read the paragraph. Then, answer the question.

There were no food-cooling systems in the 1800s. So, milk soured quickly. Louis Pasteur, a French chemist, wondered what caused it. He discovered that tiny, invisible organisms would grow in the liquid and multiply very quickly. This discovery led Pasteur to develop a way to prevent the growth of these organisms. Through experimentation, he discovered that heat, applied for a short amount of time, would destroy the organisms and keep the milk safe. Later, these organisms were called *bacteria*. The process Pasteur invented became known as *pasteurization*. It is used in the manufacturing of milk and milk products around the world.

Why was Louis Pasteur a good scientist? Write a paragraph naming three characteristics and related examples.

_____

_____

_____

_____

_____

_____

_____

_____

_____

_____

_____

_____

1. What is matter?

_____

_____

2. Think about an orange. Describe four of its physical properties.

_____

_____

Which has more mass—a potato or a potato chip? Explain.

_____

_____

Look at the pictures. Circle the picture that has more volume. Explain your choice.

_____

_____

What are the three states of matter? Give an example of each.

_____

_____

_____

Look at the pictures in Day 2. What do they show about one property of a liquid?

_____

What is a physical change? Give two examples.

_____

_____

What is a chemical change? Give two examples.

_____

_____

 0-7682-3524-3 *Science 4 Today*

Assessment # 6

Answer the questions.

1. Mason turns a plastic cup upside down and pushes it into a sink filled with water. What happens? Explain.

_____

_____

_____

2. Imagine that you have two different objects that are the same size. Do these items always have the same mass? Explain.

_____

_____

3. What is the difference in a physical change and a chemical change? Give an example of each.

_____

_____

_____

Fill in the circle next to the best answer.

4. Which is not a physical change?

   (A) heating   (C) writing

   (B) cooling   (D) tarnishing

5. When does water change from ice to a liquid?

   (A) at its melting point   (C) at its physical change

   (B) at its boiling point   (D) at its chemical change

Week #7: Force and Motion

Day #1

What is a force?

_____

Name threes ways that a force can affect an object.

_____

_____

_____

Day #2

Write a word to correctly complete each sentence.

1. A leaf falls off a tree because of the force of _____.
2. A soccer ball slows down and stops rolling because of the force of _____.
3. A book will stay on a table until it is picked up because of _____.

Answer the question.

4. Why is it harder to walk up the stairs than to walk down them?

_____

Day #3

Write *true* or *false*.

1. _____ A moving object will move in a circle.
2. _____ A force will make a moving object slow down or stop.
3. _____ An object that is not moving can sometimes move by itself.
4. _____ All objects have the ability to stay at rest or move.
5. _____ When a force is applied to an object, the object pushes back with the same amount of force.

Day #4

Draw a line to match each term with its meaning.

energy	the energy of an object because it is moving
potential energy	the energy caused by a chemical change
kinetic energy	the ability to do work
mechanical energy	the energy an object has because it can move or is moving
electrical energy	the energy that an object has because of its position
chemical energy	the energy caused by the flow of electricity

Assessment

Assessment # 7

Read each situation. Explain what kind of force is working.

1. Jean does a handstand on the gym floor.

_____

_____

2. Emilio catches a soccer ball with his hands before it flies into the net.

_____

_____

3. The brakes slow Soon Li's bike.

_____

_____

4. A roller coaster zooms down a hill.

_____

_____

5. The bat strikes the ball and sends it flying over the fence.

_____

_____

Fill in the circle next to the best answer.

6. What kind of energy will a diver have when she takes her position on the edge of a diving board?

    (A) electrical   (C) kinetic

    (B) potential   (D) chemical

What is work?

_____

_____

Sahil is pulling a wagon from the front, and Ken is pushing it from behind. The wagon is so full that is not moving. Is work being done? Explain.

_____

_____

Write the name of the simple machine being described.

1. The _____ has a flat surface where one end is higher than the other.
2. The _____ is made with a rope and wheel.
3. The _____ is made when a rod runs through a wheel.
4. The _____ is made when an inclined plane wraps around a rod.
5. The _____ has slanted sides.
6. The _____ is made when a board rests on a fulcrum.

Name one object that is an example of each simple machine.

_____

_____

_____

_____

_____

How is a compound machine like a complex machine? How are the machines different?

_____

_____

_____

_____

_____

Assessment

Assessment # 8

1. How do you know when work is being done?

    _____

    _____

    _____

2. Look around the classroom and find three examples of simple machines. List them in the chart below. Then, complete the chart.

School Object	Simple Machine	Use

3. What kind of machine is a bike? Tell how you know.

    _____

    _____

    _____

4. Is a car engine a system? Explain.

    _____

    _____

Name the three parts of an atom and the kind of charge each part has?

_____

_____

How does an object get an electric charge?

_____

_____

Label the diagram.

What does the diagram show?

_____

Explain how the current flows through the system shown above.

_____

_____

If the switch is open, what happens to the system? Explain.

_____

_____

Why are electrical wires covered in plastic? Use the words in the box in your explanation.

insulator	conductor

_____

_____

_____

_____

Assessment

Assessment # 9

Fill in the circle next to the best answer.

1. What makes an electric charge?

    (A) gaining electrons   (C) gaining negative charges

    (B) losing electrons   (D) all of the above

2. Which material is not a conductor?

    (A) glass   (C) metal

    (B) plastic   (D) water

Answer the questions.

3. Leon finishes his homework and turns off the lamp. What happens? Explain.

    _____

    _____

4. Ellen is decorating a tree with lights. When she checks the string of lights, she sees that one bulb is burned out. What kind of circuit does the string have? Explain how you know.

    _____

    _____

5. How does the use of electricity affect your daily life? Give two examples in your explanation.

    _____

    _____

    _____

    _____

    _____

What is a magnet?

_____

_____

What parts of the magnet has the greatest magnetic force?

_____

_____

Complete the sentences.

1. The ends of the magnets are called _____.

2. There is a north end and a _____ end.

3. If a magnet is tied to a string and held in the air, the north end of the magnet will point _____.

4. The unlike ends of the magnet _____ each other.

5. The like ends of the magnet _____ each other.

Look at the picture. Write **N** or **S** to label the ends of the magnets. Then, explain what is happening in the picture.

_____

_____

_____

_____

Write *true* or *false*.

1. _____ A compass is a device that has a magnetized needle.

2. _____ The needle in a compass always points south.

3. _____ Earth is a magnet that has a north and south pole.

4. _____ A needle can be made into a magnet when it is stroked in the same direction many times.

Assessment

Assessment # 10

Read the paragraph. Then, answer the questions.

In 1820, Hans Oersted was experimenting with electricity. He sent an electric current along a wire. A compass happened to be near the experiment, and Oersted noticed that the needle pointed toward the wire when the current was moving. With more experimenting, Oersted discovered that a magnetic field surrounded any conductor through which a current flowed. Five years later, William Sturgeon found that the force of the magnetic field could be increased if a piece of iron was put inside a coiled wire. It was the first electromagnet. By the end of the 1820s, Joseph Henry made a practical electromagnet. Today, huge electromagnets are built inside generators. They create electricity that powers many appliances in your house. Electromagnets are also inside your home in the form doorbells and telephones.

1. How does an electromagnet work?

_____

_____

2. Why might an electromagnet be a good source of energy for a doorbell?

_____

_____

3. Why was Hans Oersted a good scientist? Name at least two characteristics.

_____

_____

_____

4. What parts make up the system of an electromagnet?

_____

_____

Name

Listen to the sounds around you. Name three sounds that are made by natural objects and three sounds made by human-made objects.

Natural sounds: _____

_____

Human-made sounds: _____

_____

How are all sounds made? _____

Day #1

What are sound waves?

_____

How do sound waves move?

_____

_____

_____

Day #2

What is volume?

_____

_____

Why does shouting have more volume than whispering?

_____

_____

Day #3

Circle the sound wave that has a low pitch.

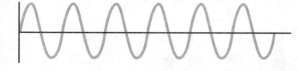

Explain why you circled the picture you did.

_____

_____

Day #4

Assessment # 11

Look at the graph. Then, answer the questions.

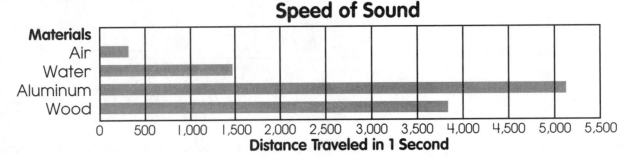

1. Through which states of matter can sound travel?

_____

2. Of the materials on the graph, through which does sound travel the fastest?

_____

3. Why might sound travel more quickly through aluminum than air?

_____

4. If you wanted to use one of the materials above to soundproof a room. Which would you choose? Explain.

_____

_____

Fill in the circle next to the best answer.

5. How does a musician pluck a string to make the volume of a guitar louder?

   Ⓐ slowly   Ⓒ quickly

   Ⓑ softly   Ⓓ hard

6. Which sound has the greatest volume?

   Ⓐ a whisper   Ⓒ a shout

   Ⓑ a washing machine   Ⓓ a jet taking off

Write a **P** in front of each characteristic of a plant.

_____ can grow

_____ made of cells

_____ needs shelter

_____ makes its own food

_____ learns behavior

_____ can reproduce

_____ gets foods from dead organisms

_____ cannot move

What are the two main groups of plants? Give two examples of each.

Group 1:_____

_____

Group 2:_____

_____

Does a daisy belong in the same main plant group as a pine tree? Explain.

_____

Label the parts of a flower. Tell what each part does.

How does moss reproduce?

_____

_____

What is pollination? Name two ways that plants are pollinated.

_____

_____

Assessment

Assessment # 12

Answer the questions.

1. Explain fertilization of a flowering plant. Use the words in the box in your explanation.

pollen pistil	ovary	sperm	egg	seed

_____

_____

_____

_____

2. How do insects pollinate flowers?

_____

_____

3. A corn plant grows two kinds of flowers. The flowers that have the stamens grow at the top of the stalk. The flowers that have the pistils grow on the rest of the stalk. How does the plant reproduce?

_____

_____

Fill in the circle next to the best answer.

4. What is the name of the process where seeds begin to grow?

(A) fertilization   (C) pollination

(B) germination   (D) classification

5. Which plant reproduces using spores?

(A) oak tree   (C) grass

(B) rose   (D) fern

Unscramble the letters in bold to make words that tell about animal characteristics.

1. Animals can grow and **druepcroe**.

2. They all must find their own **dofo**.

3. They live in a **reelths** that protects them from weather and predators.

4. Adult animals have **noyug** that look like them.

5. All animals need **nyxoge** to breathe.

What are the two main groups of animals? Give two examples of each.

Group 1:_____

_____

Group 2:_____

_____

How are a beetle and worm alike? How are they different?

_____

Animals with backbones can be classified into smaller groups, or classes. Draw a line to match each class with one of its characteristics.

fish   feeds its young milk

amphibian   its body is covered in dry scales

reptile   lives in fresh or salt water

bird   its body is covered in feathers

mammal   lives part of its life in the water and part of it on land

What is an exoskeleton? Explain its function.

_____

_____

What does it mean to be cold-blooded? Name three classes of animals having this characteristic.

_____

_____

Assessment # 13

Answer the questions.

1. What is a backbone? Explain why it is an important characteristic to scientists who study animals.

_____

_____

_____

2. Read the animal names in the box. Write each name in the correct class below.

hawk	whale	salamander	parrot	alligator
bass	shark	snake	human	frog

Fish   Amphibian   Reptile

_____ _____ _____

_____ _____ _____

Bird   Mammal

_____ _____

_____ _____

3. A butterfly and bird both have wings, and they come from eggs. Why don't they belong to the same class of animals?

_____

_____

Fill in the circle next to the best answer.

4. Which is not a characteristic of a mammal?

 Ⓐ Hair can be found on its body. Ⓒ It feeds its young milk from the female's body.

 Ⓑ It gives birth to live young. Ⓓ It is cold-blooded.

Write a word from the box to complete each definition.

trait	diversity	inherit	heredity	species

1. _____ – the passing of characteristics from one generation to the next

2. _____ – the condition of being different

3. _____ – a group of animals that can reproduce

4. _____ – a feature or characteristic gotten from a parent

5. _____ – to get a characteristic from a parent or ancestor

Day #1

Puppies look similar to the adult dogs when they are young. Yet, puppies in the same liter can look different. They may be different colors. Some may have smooth fur, while others may have rough fur. Think of other species of animals. What are two advantages for animals in a species to be different?

_____

_____

What are two disadvantages of animals in a species to be different?

_____

Day #2

Why is it important that animals inherit traits from their parents?

_____

_____

What are three specific traits that you inherited from your parents that your friends did not?

_____

_____

Day #3

A species can differ in several ways. Some animals have inherited a characteristic, but individual conditions affect its growth and development. For example, all the people in a family may be tall. The offspring will probably be tall, too. The body systems and the environment will affect just how tall, though. Think about other animals. What are two inherited characteristics that affect an organism? Explain.

_____

_____

_____

Day #4

Assessment

Assessment # 14

Answer the questions.

1. How does heredity affect a species?

_____

_____

_____

2. What are three main differences in a species? Give an example of each.

_____

_____

_____

_____

_____

_____

_____

3. Do you think it is better to have diversity in a species or not? Explain.

_____

_____

_____

_____

_____

_____

What is a behavior?

_____

Write a behavior for each organism.

dog _____

fish _____

ant _____

human being _____

Write **L** if the behavior is learned. Write **I** if the behavior is an instinct.

1. _____ A dolphin jumps through a hoop.

2. _____ A butterfly gets nectar from a flower.

3. _____ A fawn stays in the grass until called by its mother.

4. _____ A bird makes a nest.

5. _____ A lion attacks the neck of an antelope.

6. _____ A dog comes when it hears its name.

What is a reflex? Give one example.

_____

_____

How are a stimulus and a response related? Give an example.

_____

_____

What are two ways that animals learn behaviors? Give an example of each.

_____

_____

_____

_____

_____

Name

Assessment # 15

Answer the questions.

1. How do instincts help animals? Give two examples.

_____

_____

_____

2. How does a lion use both instinct and learned behaviors to get food?

_____

_____

_____

3. Give two examples of a stimulus and response relationship.

Example 1: _____

_____

Example 2: _____

_____

Fill in the circle next to the best answer.

4. What system controls reflexes?

(A) circulatory   (C) digestive

(B) nervous   (D) muscular

5. Which is a behavior that is an instinct for a baby?

(A) crying   (C) talking

(B) laughing   (D) chewing

What is the process by which plants get food energy? Identify the three things plants need in the process.

_____

How does a plant use its leaves in the process?

_____

_____

_____

Unscramble the letters in bold to make a word that completes each sentence.

1. All living things need **greeny** to survive.
2. Plants use light energy to make **guras** that they store.
3. Animals are **smonsruce** because they eat plants and other animals.
4. An **evibrroeh** is an animal that eats plants to get the stored energy of sugar.
5. A **anorvecri** is an animal that eats other animals to get the stored energy of nutrients.
6. An **ermovnio** is an animal that gets energy from both plants and animals.

What are two ways that the energy stored in dead organisms is used? Give examples of each.

_____

_____

What is the relationship between decomposers and plants?

_____

_____

Write **1** through **6** to show how energy is passed along in a food chain.

_____ spider

_____ cricket

_____ sun

_____ snake

_____ grass

_____ frog

Assessment

Assessment # 16

Answer the questions.

1. Give an example of a food chain that has at least four organisms.

_____

_____

2. Explain how human beings can harm the food chain you listed and its affects on the other living things.

_____

_____

_____

_____

3. What are some ways that human beings can help the food chain you listed?

_____

_____

_____

_____

Fill in the circle next to the best answer.

4. What is the main source of energy for plants?

   (A) sugar   (C) decomposers

   (B) nutrients   (D) oxygen

5. How is energy passed from one organism to another?

   (A) chlorophyll   (C) photosynthesis

   (B) food chains   (D) oxygen

What is an ecosystem?

_____

List three ecosystems.

_____

Choose one ecosystem you listed and name three living and three nonliving things in it.

Living: _____

Nonliving: _____

Look at the living and nonliving things you listed above. Explain how they are useful to each other.

_____

_____

_____

_____

_____

What are three changes, natural or human-made, that might happen in an ecosystem?

_____

_____

How do the above changes affect an ecosystem?

_____

_____

What is a habitat?

_____

_____

How is a habitat different from an ecosystem?

_____

_____

Assessment

Assessment # 17

Answer the questions.

1. In some towns, foxes are eating out of garbage cans instead of finding food in forests. Explain why.

_____

_____

_____

_____

2. Describe how living and nonliving things are useful to each other in a desert ecosystem.

_____

_____

_____

_____

_____

3. Imagine that you are getting a pet hamster. Explain everything you will need to make a habitat that provides for all of its needs.

_____

_____

_____

_____

_____

_____

0-7682-3524-3   *Science 4 Today*   **46**

Write *true* or *false*.

1. _____ The moon is a satellite that revolves around Earth.

2. _____ It takes exactly 29 days for the moon to circle around Earth.

3. _____ The moon makes its own light.

4. _____ The changes in the moon's shape are called *phases*.

Rewrite any false statement to make it true.

_____

Draw a line to match each phase with its description. Then, write numbers **1** through **8** to show the correct order of the moon's phases.

_____ waxing gibbous moon   The moon looks like a big, bright circle.
_____ third-quarter moon   A sliver of the shrinking moon is lit.
_____ waning gibbous moon   A sliver of the growing moon is lit.
_____ waxing crescent moon   One half of the shrinking moon is lit.
_____ first-quarter moon   The moon looks dark in the night sky.
_____ waning crescent moon   The growing moon's surface is mostly lit.
_____ new moon   One half of the growing moon is lit.
_____ full moon   The shrinking moon's surface is mostly lit.

Dan looks out at the night sky. He sees a waxing gibbous moon. Draw a circle in the diagram below to show where the moon is in relation to Earth and the sun.

 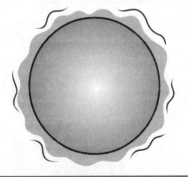

What kind of eclipse is shown in the diagram?

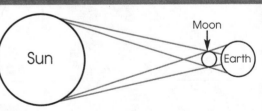

_____

Explain what is happening in this kind of eclipse.

_____

_____

Assessment

Assessment # 18

Answer the questions.

1. What is the difference in a solar and lunar eclipse?

_____

_____

_____

2. What is a new moon? Explain what it looks like and why it has this
   appearance.

_____

_____

_____

3. What is the difference in a waning crescent and waxing crescent moon?

_____

_____

4. Depak sees the moon shown below. What is the name of the moon he sees?
   Which phase of the moon will he see several nights later?

_____

5. Which phase of the moon is your nighttime sky now? Explain how you know.

_____

_____

Week #19: The Structure of Earth

Label the four layers of Earth. Write one fact about each layer.

Write a word from the box to complete each sentence.

| plates | trench | fault | landforms | mountains | mantle |

1. The crust of Earth is made up of twenty _____.
2. These plates move because of the flowing hot liquid rock underneath in the _____.
3. The movement of the plates creates many of Earth's _____.
4. Sometimes, a _____ is formed under the ocean floor when two plates crash together and one slides under the other.
5. If two plates crash together and one slides under the other where there are continents, _____ can form.
6. Two plates may grind past each other and form a _____.

Write the name of a landform to replace the words in bold.

1. The cattle grazed on the green grass on the **wide, flat area of land.** _____
2. Early pioneers often built their houses in a **low place between mountains** to be protected from harsh winds. _____
3. People who live on a small **piece of land totally surrounded by water** often make a living by fishing. _____
4. Over thousands of years, the wind and water can carve out **a deep valley with high sides.** _____
5. Sahil followed the trail up the **very high, pointed piece of land.** _____

Write a sentence using each word to show its meaning.

1. river _____
_____
2. lake _____
_____
3. ocean _____
_____
4. pond _____

Assessment # 19

Fill in the circle next to the best answer.

1. Which layer of Earth is no thicker than 20 miles?

   (A) inner core

   (B) outer core

   (C) mantle

   (D) crust

2. Where do most earthquakes occur?

   (A) at a fault

   (B) in a trench

   (C) on top of a mountain

   (D) near a lake

Answer the questions.

3. How do plates move? Describe how the movement affects Earth's surface.

   _____

   _____

   _____

   _____

4. Which landforms or water features are nearby? Describe the characteristics of the places to identify them.

   _____

   _____

   _____

   _____

What is a mineral?

_____

Write **P** in front of the properties that help scientist classify minerals.

_____ how hard it is   _____ its color

_____ how shiny it is   _____ its temperature

_____ how it breaks   _____ if it is magnetic

_____ how it smells   _____ its size

What are the three kinds of rocks? Tell how each is formed?

Category 1: _____

_____

Category 2: _____

_____

Category 3: _____

_____

Circle the word that best completes each sentence.

1. A (fossil, rock) is the remains or mark left behind by a living thing that died long ago.

2. These kinds of remains are often found in (metamorphic, sedimentary) rocks.

3. The (imprint, cast) shows the mold of something thin, like a wing or leaf.

4. Some fuels we use today, like (ore, coal), are actually fossils formed from plants that lived long ago.

What is soil made of?

_____

_____

How is soil made?

_____

_____

_____

Assessment # 20

Assessment

Answer the questions.

1. Explain the four ways that rocks are weathered to form soil.

_____

_____

_____

_____

_____

2. Why is soil important?

_____

_____

3. What kind of soil do farmers look for when choosing where to plant crops? Explain.

_____

_____

Fill in the circle next to the best answer.

4. Which kind of soil is made by decomposers?

   (A) clay   (C) humus

   (B) minerals   (D) silt

5. Tran picks up a rock that easily breaks in his hands. What kind of rock is it?

   (A) sedimentary   (C) metamorphic

   (B) volcanic   (D) igneous

Write a term from the box to complete the paragraph that describes the ocean floor.

| continental slope | shoreline | ocean basin | continental shelf | trench | ridge |

Imagine swimming in the ocean. You start at the _____, where the water and land meet. The first part of your trip is along the flat land of _____. When you see the land drop sharply, you have reached the _____. Afterward, the floor is flat and smooth again, but you are very deep, because you are on the _____. If you keep swimming, you might see a chain of mountains. The highest point of the chain is the _____. Of course, don't swim into the _____. It is the deep, narrow valley formed when two plates crashed together.

Write *true* or *false*.

1. _____ Currents are areas of moving water that flow like rivers.

2. _____ Currents throughout the ocean flow at the same rate.

3. _____ Some currents are caused by the wind.

4. _____ Water currents are mostly cold.

5. _____ They can affect the weather in a place.

What is a tide?

_____

Explain what causes a high tide.

_____

_____

_____

_____

1. What causes waves?

_____

2. Explain how waves break on land.

_____

_____

_____

Assessment # 21

Answer the questions.

1. How is the ocean a system? Give three examples of three living and nonliving things in it.

_____

_____

_____

_____

2. Choose one cycle in the ocean and describe it.

_____

_____

_____

_____

3. How is an ocean like a river? How is it different? Give two examples of each.

_____

_____

_____

_____

Write a word that correctly completes each sentence.

1. A _____ is a mountain from which melted rock flows.
2. They _____ when the pressure of heat and gas forces magma to the surface.
3. The melted rock that flows out is called _____.
4. Huge columns of clouds made of rocks, gas, and _____ flow high into the air.
5. Many volcanoes are _____, or sleeping, but may erupt someday.

Day #1

What causes an earthquake?

_____

_____

How does an earthquake change the land? Give two examples.

_____

_____

Day #2

How do floods harm the land?

_____

_____

How can some floods help the land?

_____

_____

Day #3

What is the difference in a tornado and a hurricane?

_____

_____

_____

_____

_____

Day #4

Assessment

Assessment # 22

Answer the questions.

1. Will Earth look the same 100 years from now? Explain.

_____

_____

_____

2. Scientists have many devices to track the shaking of the ground around a fault line. Why would they do this?

_____

_____

_____

3. Which is easier to predict—a tornado or a hurricane? Explain.

_____

_____

_____

4. Volcanoes formed the Hawaiian Islands long ago. In fact, lava still flows out of some volcanoes today. Scientists also watch underwater volcanoes that are erupting. What do you predict will happen to Hawaii a thousand of years from now?

_____

_____

_____

Why does air temperature rise?

_____

_____

Why is the temperature over land warmer than over water?

_____

_____

Explain how wind forms.

_____

_____

_____

What is humidity?

_____

_____

How do clouds form?

_____

_____

In May, Kim sees some big, puffy clouds high above in the blue sky. Is it a good day for her to have a picnic with friends? Explain.

_____

_____

Look at the picture. What does it show? Describe what is happening.

warm air

cold air

_____

_____

_____

_____

_____

Assessment

Assessment # 23

Answer the questions.

1. Look at the weather map. Imagine that you are a weather reporter on the news. Write what you will say in a report.

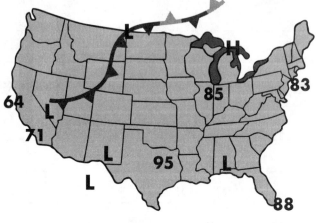

_____

_____

_____

_____

_____

_____

_____

_____

_____

2. How does weather affect your daily life? Give two examples.

_____

_____

_____

Fill in the circle next to the best answer.

3. Which is not a kind of precipitation?

    (A) sleet   (C) hail

    (B) fog   (D) rain

4. Which tool measures wind speed?

    (A) hygrometer   (C) barometer

    (B) anemometer   (D) wind vane

In 1998, Japan built the Akashi Kaiko Bridge, the longest suspension bridge. It stretches more than 12,800 feet across a busy shipping port. High winds and earthquakes frequently occur in Japan, so engineers designed the bridge with these problems in mind. The two towers, reaching nearly 930 feet into the air, have open areas so the wind will blow through. Other parts sway to balance any movement in the bridge.

Why do you think the engineers built the towers with open areas?

_____

_____

Tall buildings have been around for centuries. Many were made of thick rock walls to support the weight. Using a steel skeleton made it possible to build tall skyscrapers. Until 2004, the two Petronas Towers in Malaysia were the tallest buildings in the world. Each are 1483 feet tall, including the spire, a tall, pointed decoration. The buildings have 88 stories.

Why might steel be a better building material than rock?

_____

_____

There are tunnels everywhere under the ground. Workers build these tunnels to carry water, people, transportation, and wires. However, an engineer must carefully plan the construction. The ground must be examined and tested for the kind of rock and soil in the area. It is a slow process as workers must brace the ground above them as they dig.

What kind of rock would be the most unsafe when digging an underground tunnel? Explain.

_____

_____

Dams are the largest structures that people build. They control flooding, watering crops, and electricity. Dams are also popular places for boating, swimming, and fishing. China is in the process of building the biggest dam. When complete, the Three Gorges Dam will be 1.4 miles wide and 630 feet high. The reservoir, or lake behind it, will be about 350 miles long, allowing large ships to travel to cities far inside the country. However, there are some problems with the dam. Millions of people have been forced off their farmland and ancient temples have been flooded.

If there were no dams, what might the world be like?

_____

Assessment # 24

Answer the questions.

1. The Sears Tower, located in the United States, is about 1,450 feet. It has two television antennae that, when added to the rooftop height, make the total structure 1,729 feet tall. People work on a floor that is actually 200 feet higher than the Petronas Towers. Yet building experts still claim that the Petronas Towers are taller because the spire is part of the building design. Do you agree that the Petronas Towers are taller than the Sears tower? Explain.

_____

_____

_____

_____

_____

_____

2. How do people benefit from manmade structures? Are they always helpful? Explain.

_____

_____

_____

_____

_____

_____

_____

_____

How would you like to travel over 300 miles per hour—on land? In some countries, people are traveling this fast on maglev trains. While the cars look like those on a train, the maglev train uses electromagnets to move. The guideways that direct the train are lined with metal coils. As electricity moves along the guideways, large magnets on the underside of the car repel the magnetized coil. As a result, the train rises almost four inches above the track and glides forward.

What poles of the magnets on the train and the magnetized coils are facing each other? How do you know?

_____

Most cars on the road use gasoline or diesel fuel. Both materials are fossil fuels and in limited supply. They are expensive, too. As a result, more and more people are driving hybrid cars. Hybrid cars use both an electric motor and gasoline engine for power. The electric motor starts the engine and gets it moving when the greatest amount of power is needed. The gasoline engine takes over when the cruising speed is reached. Less energy is needed when the car is in motion.

Why is a hybrid car a good choice for city driving?

_____

_____

Scientists are researching another power source for transportation—the sun. Energy from the sun is inexhaustible and will not run out. So scientists are experimenting with placing dark solar panels on lightweight vehicles. The panels absorb the sun's light, where it is changed into electric energy. The electric energy immediately powers the wheels or remains stored in a battery for a short time. While many scientists don't think a solar car will ever be practical, they are learning much about energy.

Why do scientists think that solar cars will not be practical?

_____

Corn is a source of energy for people and animals. It is also a source of energy for some vehicles. This renewable resource is being turned into a liquid fuel by removing the starch and turning it into sugar. Known as *ethanol*, this bio-fuel burns much more cleanly and reduces the pollution in the air. It can be used in both light vehicles and heavy trucks.

List two reasons that ethanol is a good source of fuel.

_____

_____

Assessment # 25

Answer the questions.

1. How might the maglev train both help and harm the environment?

    _____

    _____

    _____

    _____

2. Name two reasons telling why people buy hybrid cars.

    _____

    _____

    _____

3. What are two important reasons that scientists are working to develop new forms of transportation?

    _____

    _____

    _____

Fill in the circle next to the best answer.

4. Which vehicle does not use electricity?

    (A) maglev train   (C) hybrid car

    (B) diesel train   (D) solar car

5. When does a hybrid use gasoline?

    (A) when it starts   (C) when it moves at a steady speed

    (B) when it begins to speed (D) when it stops

Week #26: Ocean Technology

The ocean is very deep. In some places, it is nearly 10,000 feet down to the floor. Pressure from the weight of the water, cold temperatures, and the lack of sunlight make it a dangerous place to visit. So how do scientist know so much about this ecosystem? They use *Alvin. Alvin* is the first ocean-diving vehicle that can carry several people to the bottom of the ocean. One dive especially surprised the scientists. They didn't think anything could live in the deep water. Yet, they saw tube worms and other amazing fish.

Why might scientists not expect to find living things in deep ocean water?

_____

NR-1 is a nuclear submarine that can dive in deep ocean water. It can stay there for up to a month, too. *NR-1* has mapped the ocean floor and looked for sunken ships using sonar. The ship sends out sound waves and waits for them to come back. Scientists can tell how deep something is by the time that it takes for the sound to return. *NR-1* even has a tool that can grip objects up to 2,000 pounds and pull them into the ship.

Suppose the scientists on *NR-1* send out a sound wave, and it comes back quickly. What might they conclude?

_____

Jason is a robot that explores the ocean floor. Because it is a robot, no one gets inside. *Jason* has cables that link it to computers on a ship. Scientists send information to *Jason* telling it where to go and what to videotape. *Jason* also has an arm that collects things that scientist want to see.

How is *Jason* like *NR-1*? How is it different?

_____

_____

_____

People are living in space, but did you know that they live under the water, too? Scientists have designed a four-room living area underwater that has a shower, refrigerator with frozen food, beds, and a television. Cables supply water and air to the scientists as they work. For ocean exploration, they use special air tanks, like those used by astronauts. The tanks recycle the carbon dioxide they breathe out, allowing the aquanauts to explore the ocean for longer periods of time. Past space travel has helped scientists explore other areas in our world, like the ocean. Explain how.

_____

_____

Assessment

Assessment # 26

Answer the questions.

1. Why is ocean research important? Give three reasons.

_____

_____

_____

_____

_____

_____

_____

2. Why is sonar a good tool to use in the ocean?

_____

_____

_____

3. Why might robots be more useful in ocean exploration? Give two reasons.

_____

_____

_____

_____

What is communication?

_____

_____

List four ways that people communicate.

_____

_____

How do people use a computer to communicate? List three ways.

_____

_____

_____

_____

_____

With a cell phone, people can make phone calls and receive phone calls wherever they are—at the store, at the park, or in the car. Cell phones turn the human voice into a kind of electricity. The electricity travels through the air to a cell phone tower. The tower locates the other phone and sends the electricity there. Once the electricity enters the other phone, the phone changes it back into the human voice.

What kind of phone did your parents use when they were young? How has the phone changed?

_____

If you turn on the television, you might be able choose from over 100 programs. There are two main ways that people are able to view so many programs. One way is through cable television. Wires that carry television signals run to each house. People hook their televisions to the wires. Some people may use a satellite dish to receive programs. A dish is a bowl-shaped device that attaches to the outside of a house. A satellite in space collects signals from a television station, makes them louder, and sends them back to Earth instantly.

Why might all houses not have cable television? Name two reasons.

_____

Assessment

Assessment # 27

Answer the questions.

1. How has technology changed communication in the last 100 years?

_____

_____

_____

_____

_____

_____

_____

_____

_____

_____

_____

2. List three ways that you use technology to communicate.

_____

_____

_____

_____

_____

_____

_____

Name

A robot is a device that gathers information about the environment and reacts to the information almost immediately. They are usually designed for a specific task. They may have cameras that act as eyes and sensors that pick up sound waves to hear. Scientists load information into a computer system that helps these devices work.

How is a robot like a machine? How are they different?

_____

_____

Day #1

Name two robots that you use. Tell why they are robots.

_____

_____

_____

Why do people build robots?

_____

_____

Day #2

Many factories use robots. Most robots are computers with arms that do a single task. What are two reasons that robots are a good choice for working in factories?

_____

_____

_____

_____

Day #3

Two robots were sent to Mars to explore its surface. The robots, called *rovers*, were autonomous, meaning that they reacted to things they found in the environment without direction from people. The robots rolled on the surface of Mars and took pictures. Arms could hold different tools to take samples of the soil and rocks. The information and pictures were sent to scientists on Earth.

Where else could robots be used?

_____

_____

Day #4

Assessment

Assessment # 28

Answer the questions.

1. Robots often do tasks that people do not want to do. If you could design a robot, what task would you have it do? How might this affect you and your life?

_____

_____

_____

_____

_____

_____

_____

_____

_____

_____

2. What are two reasons that robots might be harmful to society?

_____

_____

_____

_____

_____

_____

_____

Write *true* or *false*.

1. _____ The tissue is the smallest unit in an organism.

2. _____ A group of cells join together to form an organ.

3. _____ An organ is made of different tissues.

4. _____ Each organ has a job to do so the body works.

5. _____ Organs work together in a system.

Draw a line from the name of each body system to its job.

digestive   Bones support the body and give it shape.

muscular   Muscles help the body move and give it shape.

circulatory   Food is changed into energy that the body can use.

skeletal   Waste is removed from the body.

excretory   Oxygen enters the body, and carbon dioxide leaves the body.

nervous   The brain and nerves control the whole body.

Write **C** if the sentence tells about the circulatory system.

_____ Nutrients travel by blood to the cells in the body.

_____ Juices break down the food into nutrients.

_____ It helps fight infections.

_____ It removes leftover food wastes.

_____ It controls body temperature.

_____ Oxygen moves all over your body.

Explain how the respiratory system works. Use the words in the box in your explanation.

| lungs | nose | mouth | trachea | alveoli |

_____

_____

_____

_____

Assessment # 29

Answer the questions.

What body system is shown below? Write the name of the system. Then, label the diagram. Briefly explain the function of each organ.

Body system: _____

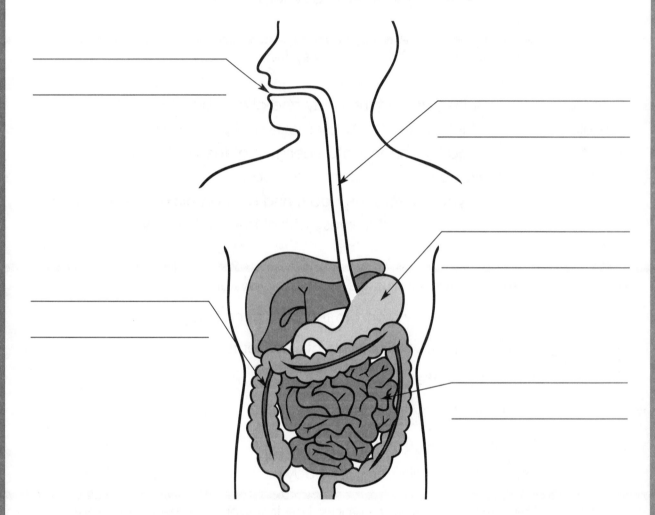

Are all parts in a human body system important? Explain.

_____

_____

_____

_____

70

Write three foods that belong in each food group.

Grains: _____

Vegetables: _____

Fruits: _____

Milk: _____

Meat and Beans: _____

Why is it important to eat a healthy diet? Give two reasons.

_____

_____

_____

Why should you eat foods of all different colors?

_____

_____

Name three ways that exercise helps the body.

_____

_____

_____

_____

_____

Read the label. Is this a healthy snack? Explain.

_____

_____

_____

_____

_____

Nutrition Facts	
Serving Size: 1 bag • 1.75 oz	
Amount Per Serving	
Calories 280 Calories from Fat 162	
Total Fat 18g	28%
Cholesterol 0mg	0%
Sodium 340mg	14%
Total Carbohydrate 25g	8%
Protein 3g	6%

Day #1

Day #2

Day #3

Day #4

Assessment

Assessment # 30

Fill in the circle next to the best answer.

1. Why do bike riders wear helmets?

   (A) It protects their brain in an accident.

   (B) It plays music.

   (C) It keeps their head warm.

   (D) All of the above.

2. Why should you brush your teeth after eating?

   (A) to get rid of the food taste   (C) to remove bacteria

   (B) to make the gums pink   (D) to help bacteria grow

3. Why should you cover your mouth when you cough?

   (A) so people can't see the germs   (C) to make the germs go away

   (B) to keep germs from spreading   (D) to develop more germs

4. Which group of foods is an example of a healthy lunch?

   (A) an apple, an orange, and juice

   (B) turkey sandwich on wheat bread, kiwi, and milk

   (C) ham sandwich on white bread, chips, and yogurt

   (D) broccoli, carrots, and milk

Answer the question.

5. List two hygiene habits you do daily. Explain why each is important.

_____

_____

_____

_____

Write a word to correctly complete each sentence.

1. Adding harmful materials to the environment causes _____.
2. Dumping trash on the ground results in _____ pollution.
3. Construction sights using heavy equipment and loud music produce _____ pollution.
4. Sewage and oil leaks into ponds, lakes, streams, and oceans make _____ pollution.
5. The _____ pollution is a huge problem because it affects our breathing and temperature balance on Earth.
6. People are also concerned about _____ pollution in big cities because bright lights make it difficult to see the stars at night.

Day #1

List three causes of air pollution.

_____

_____

_____

How does air pollution affect plants?

_____

_____

Day #2

List three causes of water pollution.

_____

_____

_____

How does water pollution affect animals?

_____

_____

Day #3

Most of what people throw away ends up in landfills. What problem arises when it rains near some landfills?

_____

What is one way that communities reuse landfills? How does this help the community?

_____

_____

Day #4

Assessment # 31

Assessment

Look at the graph. Then, answer the questions.

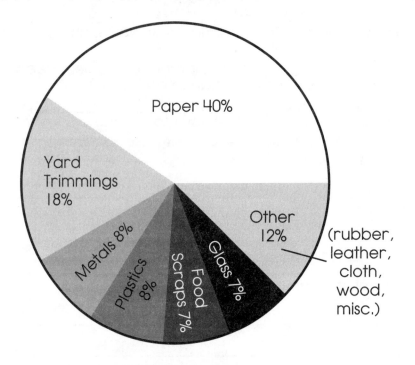

1. Which kind of trash is thrown out the most?

   _____

2. What are three examples of this kind of trash that you throw out?

   _____

3. Tell one way that you can reduce the waste in three of the above categories.

   _____

   _____

   _____

   _____

   _____

What is the greenhouse effect?

_____

_____

Why is this system important to Earth?

_____

_____

What does the picture show?

_____

_____

_____

How does this affect nature?

_____

What is global warming?

_____

_____

List three specific causes of global warming.

_____

_____

_____

What is the main effect of global warming?

_____

List three ways that the balance of nature is affected by global warming.

_____

_____

_____

Assessment

Assessment # 32

Answer the questions.

1. How does the greenhouse effect affect the balance of nature?

_____

_____

_____

_____

_____

_____

_____

_____

_____

2. What are three things that you can do to reduce global warming?

_____

_____

_____

_____

_____

_____

_____

Day #1

What is a natural resource?

_____

_____

Write **R** beside each item that is a natural resource.

_____ air   _____ corn   _____ water

_____ cow   _____ rock   _____ coal

_____ shirt   _____ electricity   _____ paper

Day #2

What is a renewable resource? Give two examples.

_____

_____

What is an inexhaustible resource? Give two examples.

_____

_____

Day #3

Where are most nonrenewable resources found?

_____

_____

Should nonrenewable resources be used carefully? Explain.

_____

_____

_____

Day #4

What are three ways that people can help conserve natural resources?

_____

_____

_____

_____

Assessment # 33

Assessment

Answer the questions.

1. What is petroleum? Where is it found?

_____

_____

2. Why is petroleum a renewable resource?

_____

_____

3. Should petroleum be conserved? Explain.

_____

_____

_____

Fill in the circle next to the best answer:

4. What kind of resource is water?

  (A) exhaustible

  (B) inexhaustible

  (C) renewable

  (D) nonrenewable

5. How does a lumber company make sure that trees are a renewable resource?

  (A) They don't cut too many trees.

  (B) They make less paper products.

  (C) They plant trees in places they log.

  (D) They only cut in rain forests.

Draw a line to match each word to its meaning.

ecosystem   the place an animal lives where all its needs can be met

habitat   all the populations that live in a place

population   all the living and nonliving things in a place

environment   a group of one kind of living thing that lives in a place

community   everything that is around a living thing

Why do scientists keep track of populations? Explain.

_____

_____

Animals often move around. How might scientist keep track of the animals in these populations?

_____

_____

A scientist made a graph to show the changing populations of rabbits and coyotes in a park. Look at the graph. Then, answer the questions.

What happened to the rabbit population for the first six years?

_____

When did the coyote population begin to increase?

_____

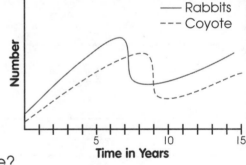

Look at the graph above. What can you conclude about the relationship of the rabbit and coyote populations? Explain.

_____

_____

_____

_____

_____

Assessment # 34

Answer the questions.

1. What are three reasons that a population might change?

   _____

   _____

   _____

2. Look at the food chain below. Suppose a disease strikes the mice. Explain what might happen to each remaining organism in the food chain.

   _____

   _____

   _____

   _____

Fill in the circle next to the best answer.

3. Which animal is extinct?

   (A) eagle   (C) dinosaur

   (B) grizzly bear   (D) A and C

4. Which is a factor that could affect a population?

   (A) reproduction rate   (C) disease

   (B) climate   (D) all of the above

Unscramble the letters in bold to make a word that completes each sentence.

1. People practice **rasncoonitev** when they protect and use natural resources wisely.
2. Some animal populations, like the dinosaurs, are **cixtent**.
3. Other populations are **gadneenerd**, meaning there are few of them left.
4. Scientists, the government, and many people work together to **torcept** these organisms.
5. They put aside land as a **furege** where the plants and animals can live in safety.

Circle the picture that shows the plowing method that will best conserve the soil. Explain why a farmer would do this.

_____

_____

_____

Why are forests important? Name two reasons.

_____

_____

In many forests, lumber companies are supposed to plant new trees to replace the ones they cut. Why?

_____

_____

Why are some animals endangered? Name two reasons.

_____

_____

Why do people protect endangered animals?

_____

_____

Day #1

Day #2

Day #3

Day #4

Assessment # 35

Answer the question.

More than half of all plants and animal species in the world live in the rain forest. Scientists believe that millions more exist, but have not yet been discovered. However, in the last fifty years, nearly half of the rain forests have been destroyed. Why is the rain forest ecosystem important? What are people doing to save it?

_____

_____

_____

_____

_____

_____

_____

_____

_____

_____

_____

_____

_____

_____

_____

_____

_____

_____

Week #36: Roman Contributions

The Romans lived over two thousand years ago. They developed many ideas that we use today. For example, the Romans wanted their rooms to stay warm without having a smoky fire. When building, workers stacked piles of stones on the floor. Then, they built another floor on top, leaving a space between the two. They also built two walls that had spaces between them. Slaves made a huge fire in one of the spaces. The warm air would move through the empty spaces and blew through holes into the rooms.

What system do we use today that is like the one described above? Explain.

_____

_____

Day #1

The Romans built huge cities for people to live in. They needed large amounts of water, but a supply was not available nearby. The Romans designed aqueducts to carry water from a distant water source. They joined arches together, sometimes stacked several stories high, and formed a U-shaped channel on top. The structure was sloped down toward the city so that the water would keep flowing.

How did the Romans use physics to help them get water?

_____

_____

Day #2

Human waste could have been a problem for so many people living close together. The Romans designed a system to get rid of it. They dug tunnels underground to carry the dirty water and wastes. The Romans built drains in their houses. All sewage was poured down the drain and flowed away.

Why would the Romans want to get rid of sewage?

_____

_____

_____

Day #3

Two thousand years ago, most people used stones or wood to build structures. The Romans wanted to build really big buildings. They couldn't do it with the natural resources they had, so they invented concrete. Concrete was made from small stones, water, and a binding agent, like chalk or volcanic ash. It helped them build huge and very strong structures. The finished texture wasn't pretty, so the Romans decorated the outside with pretty materials.

Why was concrete a better building material than large stone blocks?

_____

_____

Day #4

Assessment

Assessment # 36

Answer the questions.

1. The Romans had great military power. Their huge armies marched all over the land. They took wagons and catapults with them. As a result, they built a huge network of very straight roads. What two problems did the Romans solve with all these the roads?

_____

_____

_____

2. Choose one Roman contribution. How does it affect your daily life?

_____

_____

_____

Fill in the circle next to the best answer.

3. Which system did the Roman culture borrow from another culture?

(A) concrete

(B) heating

(C) roads

(D) arches

4. What carries water into houses today?

(A) aqueducts

(B) pipes

(C) drains

(D) sewers

The ancient Chinese drew pictures and wrote about their lives long before anyone else. While learning about the culture is interesting, the material they used to tell the stories is even more interesting—paper! The Chinese invented paper. They first used bamboo sticks tied together. Then, they used silk, which was expensive. Finally, one man experimented with hemp, fishing nets, rags, and bark, which led to a process to make paper.

Why was the inventor of paper a good scientist?

_____

_____

The invention of paper led to other discoveries, including ink, wood, or clay tablets to print letters and pictures, and finally the printing press. Before the printing press, only the very rich had books. They hired artists to write books that told the stories and ideas that were important to their culture. The printing press allowed workers to make many copies of the same book cheaply.

How could having the technology to print many books change a society?

_____

_____

A compass is a device that tells direction. It was very useful to sailors long ago as they traveled on the oceans. It is also a Chinese invention. People rubbed a needle on lodestone, a kind of magnetic rock. When placed in water or tied to a string, it pointed south, which was China's closest magnetic pole.

How did the compass affect history?

_____

_____

_____

Gunpowder is another Chinese invention. One of their early books tells that the Chinese had things called *fire trees* and *silver flowers*, which scientist think were fireworks. Other books tell of how the Chinese used an exploding material on an army who marched into their land.

What properties of gunpowder helped the Chinese find a new use for it? Explain.

_____

_____

_____

Assessment

Assessment # 37

Answer the questions.

1. List ten products made with paper.

_____

_____

_____

_____

2. What would your life be like without paper?

_____

_____

_____

_____

3. With the exception of paper, which Chinese invention do you think has affected history the most? Explain.

_____

_____

_____

_____

_____

_____

_____

_____

Around 1780, Joseph Montgolfier saw smoke rising from a fire. It made him wonder if the smoke could lift something. Montgolfier and his brother held opened paper bags over a fire. They filled with smoke and air, but did not rise very much. Through other experiments, the brothers discovered that it was the hot air that things rise. The discovery led the Montgolfier brothers to build the first hot air balloon. A duck, sheep, and rooster became the first passengers in 1783.

What hypothesis might Joseph Montgolfier have made when he saw the smoke rise?

_____

Wilber and Orville Wright enjoyed reading about men who flew gliders. The brothers thought they could make a better flying machine. They began to read books about flying. They experimented with different glider designs and steering devices. Then the Wright brothers added an engine to the glider. In 1903, after many experiments, the Wright brothers flew a machine for 59 seconds.

How did experimenting with different designs help the Wright brothers?

_____

_____

The helicopter was the first flying machine man thought about. An ancient Chinese toy and drawings by an artist in the late 1400s show such a device. The first helicopter was really built in the 1900s. It tipped over a lot. It wasn't until 1939 that someone made a helicopter that really worked. The inventor made the body smaller and tail longer. He also added a blade to the end of the tail.

Are failures an important part of the scientific method? Explain.

_____

_____

As early as 1903, scientists were thinking about using rockets to travel up to space. It wasn't until 1957 that the first unmanned space rocket orbited around Earth. In 1961, the first man made a trip around Earth. After that, many people traveled into space. Finally, in 1969, two Americans, Neil Armstrong and Buzz Aldrin, walked on the moon.

Why was exploring space important?

_____

_____

Assessment

Assessment # 38

Complete the page.

1. Use the information from the week to complete a time line to show the history of flight.

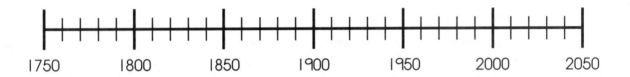

2. How might a scientist use a timeline?

_____

_____

3. How does nature affect the development of technology? Give two examples.

_____

_____

_____

_____

Write *true* or *false*.

4. _____ The Montgolfier brothers used smoke to lift the first balloon off the ground.

5. _____ The first passengers to fly were a rooster, duck, and sheep.

6. _____ Gliders were modeled on the Wright brothers' airplane.

7. _____ The first successful helicopter used two blades.

What is a cycle?

_____

Write **C** beside each cycle in nature.

_____ a volcano erupting   _____ the rain

_____ a day   _____ the soil

_____ a frog's growth   _____ petroleum

_____ a flowing river   _____ tides

What cycle is shown? Write **1** through **5** to show the order.

Cycle name: _____

_____   _____   _____   _____   _____

Explain the water cycle.

_____

_____

_____

Why is the water cycle important?

_____

_____

Think about the cycle of the seasons and the life cycle of organisms. How are they related? Give an example.

_____

_____

_____

_____

Assessment

Assessment # 39

Fill in the circle next to the best answer.

1. Ellen sees a cocoon. What part of the butterfly life cycle does she see?

    (A) egg   (C) caterpillar

    (B) pupa   (D) butterfly

2. Mark looks at the moon and sees this shape. What phase does he see?

    (A) waxing gibbous   (C) three-quarter moon

    (B) new moon   (D) waning crescent

3. Why do organisms have life cycles?

    (A) to reproduce   (C) to grow

    (B) to eat   (D) to sense

Answer the question.

4. What is another cycle in nature that has not been identified this week? Choose one, describe it, and explain its importance in nature.

_____

_____

_____

_____

_____

_____

Name

What is an inventor?

_____

_____

Name one inventor. Tell what the person invented and tell how it was useful.

_____

_____

Day #1

Brandon Whale's mother had a pacemaker implanted in her heart. She wore a device on her arm that sent signals through the telephone about her heart to a doctor's office. The device did not fit well, so the signals were not always clear. At the age of eight, Whale came up with a better design so the device fit more like a bracelet. He called it the _PaceMate_. It not only helped his mother, but it helped many other people, too.

Why did Brandon Whale invent the PaceMate?

_____

_____

Day #2

Brandon Whale's brother is also an inventor. On visits to the hospital, six-year-old Spencer Whale saw sick children with IVs in their arms trying to ride in toy cars. Parents rolled the IV poles behind the children. Sometimes, the parents tripped over the poles and pulled out the tubes. Spencer Whale decided to attach the IV poles to toy cars. Children could sit inside the cars and ride around the hospital on their own.

What two characteristics made Spencer Whale a good inventor?

_____

_____

Day #3

At the age of ten, Taylor Hernandez invented Magic Sponge Blocks. The large building blocks are made of soft sponges. Magnets inside the sponges keep the blocks stacked. When not in use, the blocks can be pressed flat like pancakes for easy storage.

Why are Hernandez's blocks a good invention? Give two reasons.

_____

_____

_____

Day #4

Assessment

Assessment # 40

Fill in the circle that best answers the question.

1. Why are Magic Sponge Blocks a good invention?

   (A) They look like pancakes.

   (B) They will not hurt children if they fall.

   (C) A kid invented them.

   (D) Magnets are fun toys.

2. Which is a characteristic of a good inventor?

   (A) observant

   (B) cautious

   (C) quick

   (D) selfish

Answer the questions.

3. Is an inventor a scientist? Explain.

   _____

   _____

   _____

4. Many inventions are made to solve a problem. Think of a problem you would like to solve. Design an invention for it. Explain the invention below and tell how it solves the problem.

   _____

   _____

   _____

   _____

Answer Key

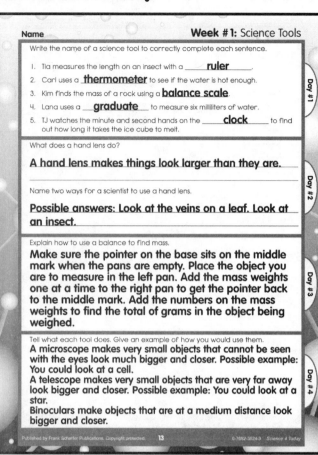

Name

Week #1: Science Tools

Write the name of a science tool to correctly complete each sentence.

Day #1

1. Tia measures the length on an insect with a ___**ruler**___.
2. Carl uses a ___**thermometer**___ to see if the water is hot enough.
3. Kim finds the mass of a rock using a ___**balance scale**___.
4. Lana uses a ___**graduate**___ to measure six milliliters of water.
5. TJ watches the minute and second hands on the ___**clock**___ to find out how long it takes the ice cube to melt.

What does a hand lens do?

Day #2

A hand lens makes things look larger than they are.

Name two ways for a scientist to use a hand lens.

Possible answers: Look at the veins on a leaf. Look at an insect.

Explain how to use a balance to find mass.

Day #3

Make sure the pointer on the base sits on the middle mark when the pans are empty. Place the object you are to measure in the left pan. Add the mass weights one at a time to the right pan to get the pointer back to the middle mark. Add the numbers on the mass weights to find the total of grams in the object being weighed.

Tell what each tool does. Give an example of how you would use them.

Day #4

A microscope makes very small objects that cannot be seen with the eyes look much bigger and closer. Possible example: You could look at a cell.
A telescope makes very small objects that are very far away look bigger and closer. Possible example: You could look at a star.
Binoculars make objects that are at a medium distance look bigger and closer.

Name

Week #1: Science Tools

Assessment

Assessment # 1

Fill in the circle next to the best answer.

1. What does a spring scale measure?
   - (A) volume
   - ● force
   - (B) mass
   - (D) length

2. Which units are on a ruler?
   - (A) degrees
   - (C) minutes
   - (B) grams
   - ● centimeters

Answer the questions.

3. Why would a scientist use a camera?

Possible answer: A camera takes a picture to show what something looks like.

4. Why is the computer an important tool? Tell three ways that a scientist could use it.

Answers will vary.

Name

Week #2: The Metric System

Day #1

What is the customary system of measurement?
Possible answer: The customary system uses feet and inches to measure length, pounds to measure weight, cups to measure capacity, and Fahrenheit degrees to measure temperature.
The metric system is based on tens. It uses centimeters and millimeters to measure length, grams to measure mass, liters to measure volume, and Celsius degrees to measure temperature.

What measurement system is used in the science community?

Day #2

The metric system is used in the science community.

Why do all scientists use this system?

Possible answer: The metric system allows scientists all around the world to understand the data gathered, even if they do not speak the same language.

Write the abbreviation for each metric measurement word.

Day #3

1. liter ___**L**___
2. gram ___**g**___
3. meter ___**m**___
4. centimeter ___**cm**___
5. milliliter ___**mL**___
6. kilogram ___**kg**___
7. millimeter ___**mm**___
8. decigram ___**dg**___
9. kilometer ___**km**___

Convert the measurements to make each equation true.

Day #4

1. 1 L = ___**1,000**___ mL
2. 1 g = ___**100**___ cg
3. 1 m = ___**1,000**___ mm
4. 10 mg = ___**0.01**___ g
5. 100 cL = ___**1000**___ mL
6. 0.1 m = ___**10**___ cm
7. 10 cg = ___**100**___ mg
8. 10 L = ___**1,000**___ cL

Name

Week #2: The Metric System

Assessment

Assessment # 2

Fill in the circle next to the best answer.

1. About what temperature is a popsicle?
   - ● –5°C
   - (C) 20°C
   - (B) 10°C
   - (D) 32°C

2. About how long is a bee?
   - (A) 2 m
   - (C) 2 mm
   - ● 2 cm
   - (D) 2 km

Write the name of an object that is about the size of each measurement.

3. 8 centimeters   **Possible answer: a crayon**
4. 1 meter   **Possible answer: the height of a desk**
5. 1 liter   **Possible answer: a bottle of water**
6. 100 milliliters   **Possible answer: a can of soup**
7. 1 gram   **Possible answer: a paper clip**

Answer the question.

8. Antone jumped 9 meters, and Wes jumped 1,000 centimeters. Who jumped farther? Explain.

Wes jumped farther. 1,000 centimeters converts to 10 meters. 10 meters is farther than 9 meters.

Answer Key

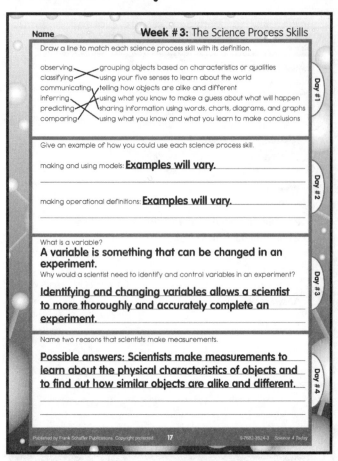

Draw a line to match each science process skill with its definition.

observing — using your five senses to learn about the world
classifying — grouping objects based on characteristics or qualities
communicating — telling how objects are alike and different
inferring — using what you know to make a guess about what will happen
predicting — sharing information using words, charts, diagrams, and graphs
comparing — using what you know and what you learn to make conclusions

Day #1

Give an example of how you could use each science process skill.

making and using models: **Examples will vary.**

making operational definitions: **Examples will vary.**

Day #2

What is a variable?
A variable is something that can be changed in an experiment.

Why would a scientist need to identify and control variables in an experiment?

Identifying and changing variables allows a scientist to more thoroughly and accurately complete an experiment.

Day #3

Name two reasons that scientists make measurements.

Possible answers: Scientists make measurements to learn about the physical characteristics of objects and to find out how similar objects are alike and different.

Day #4

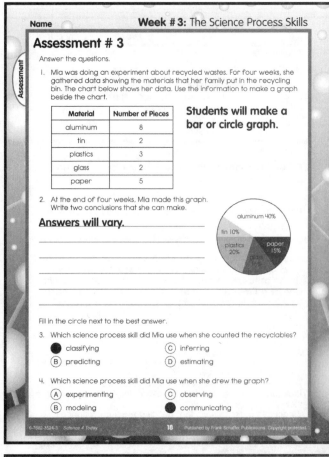

Assessment # 3

Answer the questions.

1. Mia was doing an experiment about recycled wastes. For four weeks, she gathered data showing the materials that her family put in the recycling bin. The chart below shows her data. Use the information to make a graph beside the chart.

Material	Number of Pieces
aluminum	8
tin	2
plastics	3
glass	2
paper	5

Students will make a bar or circle graph.

2. At the end of four weeks, Mia made this graph. Write two conclusions that she can make.

Answers will vary.

aluminum 40%
tin 10%
plastics 20%
paper 15%

Fill in the circle next to the best answer.

3. Which science process skill did Mia use when she counted the recyclables?
- ● classifying
- Ⓑ predicting
- Ⓒ inferring
- Ⓓ estimating

4. Which science process skill did Mia use when she drew the graph?
- Ⓐ experimenting
- Ⓑ modeling
- Ⓒ observing
- ● communicating

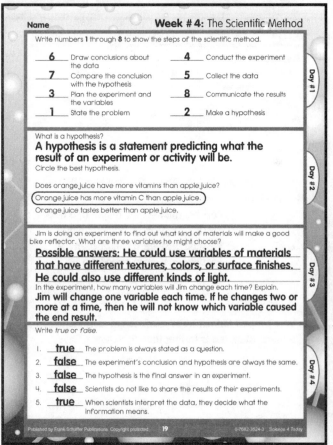

Write numbers 1 through 8 to show the steps of the scientific method.

__6__ Draw conclusions about the data
__7__ Compare the conclusion with the hypothesis
__3__ Plan the experiment and the variables
__1__ State the problem
__4__ Conduct the experiment
__5__ Collect the data
__8__ Communicate the results
__2__ Make a hypothesis

Day #1

What is a hypothesis?
A hypothesis is a statement predicting what the result of an experiment or activity will be.

Circle the best hypothesis.

Does orange juice have more vitamins than apple juice?
(Orange juice has more vitamin C than apple juice.)
Orange juice tastes better than apple juice.

Day #2

Jim is doing an experiment to find out what kind of materials will make a good bike reflector. What are three variables he might choose?
Possible answers: He could use variables of materials that have different textures, colors, or surface finishes. He could also use different kinds of light.

In the experiment, how many variables will Jim change each time? Explain.
Jim will change one variable each time. If he changes two or more at a time, then he will not know which variable caused the end result.

Day #3

Write true or false.

1. __true__ The problem is always stated as a question.
2. __false__ The experiment's conclusion and hypothesis are always the same.
3. __false__ The hypothesis is the final answer in an experiment.
4. __false__ Scientists do not like to share the results of their experiments.
5. __true__ When scientists interpret the data, they decide what the information means.

Day #4

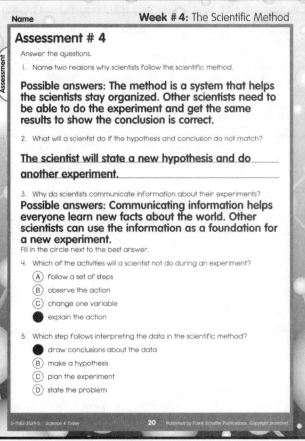

Assessment # 4

Answer the questions.

1. Name two reasons why scientists follow the scientific method.
Possible answers: The method is a system that helps the scientists stay organized. Other scientists need to be able to do the experiment and get the same results to show the conclusion is correct.

2. What will a scientist do if the hypothesis and conclusion do not match?
The scientist will state a new hypothesis and do another experiment.

3. Why do scientists communicate information about their experiments?
Possible answers: Communicating information helps everyone learn new facts about the world. Other scientists can use the information as a foundation for a new experiment.

Fill in the circle next to the best answer.

4. Which of the activities will a scientist not do during an experiment?
- Ⓐ follow a set of steps
- Ⓑ observe the action
- Ⓒ change one variable
- ● explain the action

5. Which step follows interpreting the data in the scientific method?
- ● draw conclusions about the data
- Ⓑ make a hypothesis
- Ⓒ plan the experiment
- Ⓓ state the problem

Answer Key

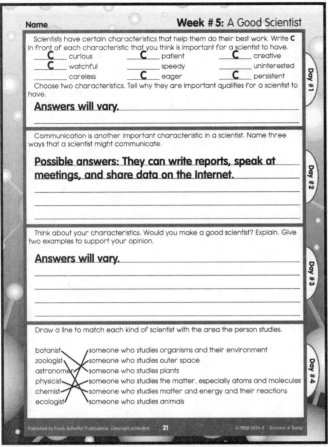

Scientists have certain characteristics that help them do their best work. Write **C** in front of each characteristic that you think is important for a scientist to have.

  C   curious   **C**   patient   **C**   creative
  C   watchful   speedy   uninterested
     careless   **C**   eager   **C**   persistent

Choose two characteristics. Tell why they are important qualities for a scientist to have.

Answers will vary.

Day #1

Communication is another important characteristic in a scientist. Name three ways that a scientist might communicate.

Possible answers: They can write reports, speak at meetings, and share data on the Internet.

Day #2

Think about your characteristics. Would you make a good scientist? Explain. Give two examples to support your opinion.

Answers will vary.

Day #3

Draw a line to match each kind of scientist with the area the person studies.

botanist — someone who studies organisms and their environment
zoologist — someone who studies outer space
astronomer — someone who studies plants
physicist — someone who studies the matter, especially atoms and molecules
chemist — someone who studies matter and energy and their reactions
ecologist — someone who studies animals

Day #4

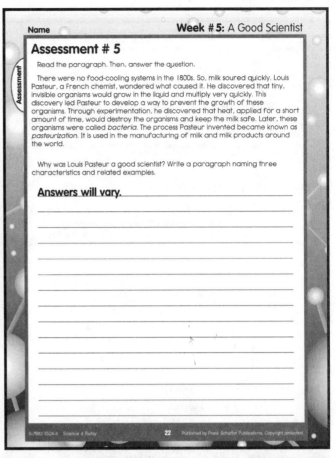

Assessment

Assessment # 5

Read the paragraph. Then, answer the question.

There were no food-cooling systems in the 1800s. So, milk soured quickly. Louis Pasteur, a French chemist, wondered what caused it. He discovered that tiny, invisible organisms would grow in the liquid and multiply very quickly. This discovery led Pasteur to develop a way to prevent the growth of these organisms. Through experimentation, he discovered that heat, applied for a short amount of time, would destroy the organisms and keep the milk safe. Later, these organisms were called *bacteria*. The process Pasteur invented became known as *pasteurization*. It is used in the manufacturing of milk and milk products around the world.

Why was Louis Pasteur a good scientist? Write a paragraph naming three characteristics and related examples.

Answers will vary.

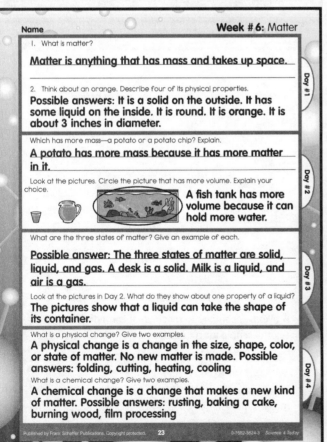

1. What is matter?

Matter is anything that has mass and takes up space.

2. Think about an orange. Describe four of its physical properties.

Possible answers: It is a solid on the outside. It has some liquid on the inside. It is round. It is orange. It is about 3 inches in diameter.

Day #1

Which has more mass—a potato or a potato chip? Explain.

A potato has more mass because it has more matter in it.

Look at the pictures. Circle the picture that has more volume. Explain your choice.

A fish tank has more volume because it can hold more water.

Day #2

What are the three states of matter? Give an example of each.

Possible answer: The three states of matter are solid, liquid, and gas. A desk is a solid. Milk is a liquid, and air is a gas.

Look at the pictures in Day 2. What do they show about one property of a liquid?

The pictures show that a liquid can take the shape of its container.

Day #3

What is a physical change? Give two examples.

A physical change is a change in the size, shape, color, or state of matter. No new matter is made. Possible answers: folding, cutting, heating, cooling

What is a chemical change? Give two examples.

A chemical change is a change that makes a new kind of matter. Possible answers: rusting, baking a cake, burning wood, film processing

Day #4

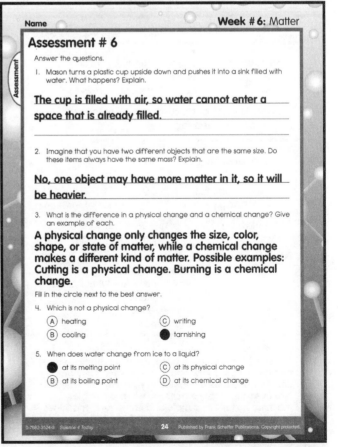

Assessment

Assessment # 6

Answer the questions.

1. Mason turns a plastic cup upside down and pushes it into a sink filled with water. What happens? Explain.

The cup is filled with air, so water cannot enter a space that is already filled.

2. Imagine that you have two different objects that are the same size. Do these items always have the same mass? Explain.

No, one object may have more matter in it, so it will be heavier.

3. What is the difference in a physical change and a chemical change? Give an example of each.

A physical change only changes the size, color, shape, or state of matter, while a chemical change makes a different kind of matter. Possible examples: Cutting is a physical change. Burning is a chemical change.

Fill in the circle next to the best answer.

4. Which is not a physical change?
   Ⓐ heating   Ⓒ writing
   Ⓑ cooling   ● tarnishing

5. When does water change from ice to a liquid?
   ● at its melting point   Ⓒ at its physical change
   Ⓑ at its boiling point   Ⓓ at its chemical change

Answer Key

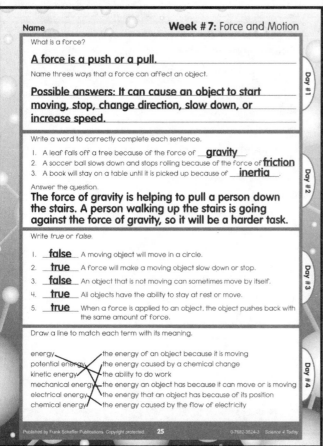

Week #7: Force and Motion

Name

Day #1

What is a force?

A force is a push or a pull.

Name threes ways that a force can affect an object.

Possible answers: It can cause an object to start moving, stop, change direction, slow down, or increase speed.

Day #2

Write a word to correctly complete each sentence.

1. A leaf falls off a tree because of the force of **gravity**.
2. A soccer ball slows down and stops rolling because of the force of **friction**.
3. A book will stay on a table until it is picked up because of **inertia**.

Answer the question.

The force of gravity is helping to pull a person down the stairs. A person walking up the stairs is going against the force of gravity, so it will be a harder task.

Day #3

Write *true* or *false*.

1. **false** A moving object will move in a circle.
2. **true** A force will make a moving object slow down or stop.
3. **false** An object that is not moving can sometimes move by itself.
4. **true** All objects have the ability to stay at rest or move.
5. **true** When a force is applied to an object, the object pushes back with the same amount of force.

Day #4

Draw a line to match each term with its meaning.

energy — the ability to do work
potential energy — the energy of an object because it is moving
kinetic energy — the energy an object has because it can move or is moving
mechanical energy — the energy that an object has because of its position
electrical energy — the energy caused by a chemical change
chemical energy — the energy caused by the flow of electricity

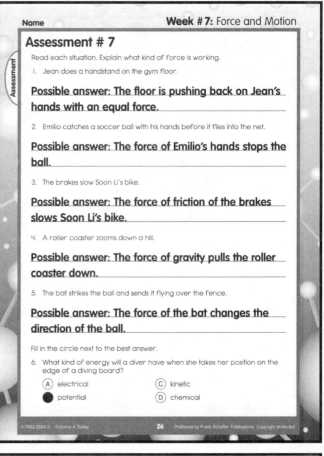

Week #7: Force and Motion

Name

Assessment

Assessment # 7

Read each situation. Explain what kind of force is working.

1. Jean does a handstand on the gym floor.

Possible answer: The floor is pushing back on Jean's hands with an equal force.

2. Emilio catches a soccer ball with his hands before it flies into the net.

Possible answer: The force of Emilio's hands stops the ball.

3. The brakes slow Soon Li's bike.

Possible answer: The force of friction of the brakes slows Soon Li's bike.

4. A roller coaster zooms down a hill.

Possible answer: The force of gravity pulls the roller coaster down.

5. The bat strikes the ball and sends it flying over the fence.

Possible answer: The force of the bat changes the direction of the ball.

Fill in the circle next to the best answer.

6. What kind of energy will a diver have when she takes her position on the edge of a diving board?
   - (A) electrical
   - (C) kinetic
   - ● potential
   - (D) chemical

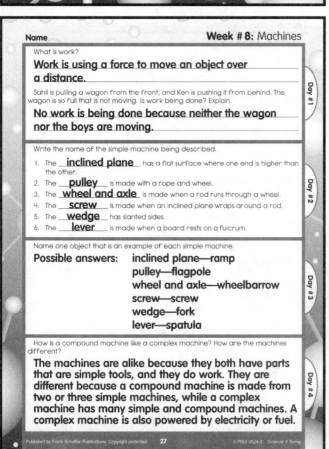

Week #8: Machines

Name

Day #1

What is work?

Work is using a force to move an object over a distance.

Sahil is pulling a wagon from the front, and Ken is pushing it from behind. The wagon is so full that is not moving. Is work being done? Explain.

No work is being done because neither the wagon nor the boys are moving.

Day #2

Write the name of the simple machine being described.

1. The **inclined plane** has a flat surface where one end is higher than the other.
2. The **pulley** is made with a rope and wheel.
3. The **wheel and axle** is made when a rod runs through a wheel.
4. The **screw** is made when an inclined plane wraps around a rod.
5. The **wedge** has slanted sides.
6. The **lever** is made when a board rests on a fulcrum.

Day #3

Name one object that is an example of each simple machine.

Possible answers: inclined plane—ramp
pulley—flagpole
wheel and axle—wheelbarrow
screw—screw
wedge—fork
lever—spatula

Day #4

How is a compound machine like a complex machine? How are the machines different?

The machines are alike because they both have parts that are simple tools, and they do work. They are different because a compound machine is made from two or three simple machines, while a complex machine has many simple and compound machines. A complex machine is also powered by electricity or fuel.

Week #8: Machines

Name

Assessment

Assessment # 8

1. How do you know when work is being done?

Something moves when it is pushed or pulled.

2. Look around the classroom and find three examples of simple machines. List them in the chart below. Then, complete the chart.

School Object	Simple Machine	Use
	Answers will vary.	

3. What kind of machine is a bike? Tell how you know.

A bike is a compound machine. It is made from several simple machines.

4. Is a car engine a system? Explain.

Yes, a car engine is made of many different parts that make it move.

Answer Key

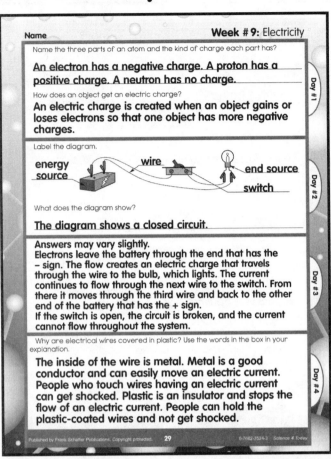

Day #1

Name the three parts of an atom and the kind of charge each part has?

An electron has a negative charge. A proton has a positive charge. A neutron has no charge.

How does an object get an electric charge?

An electric charge is created when an object gains or loses electrons so that one object has more negative charges.

Day #2

Label the diagram.

energy source   wire   end source   switch

What does the diagram show?

The diagram shows a closed circuit.

Day #3

Answers may vary slightly.
Electrons leave the battery through the end that has the – sign. The flow creates an electric charge that travels through the wire to the bulb, which lights. The current continues to flow through the next wire to the switch. From there it moves through the third wire and back to the other end of the battery that has the + sign.
If the switch is open, the circuit is broken, and the current cannot flow throughout the system.

Day #4

Why are electrical wires covered in plastic? Use the words in the box in your explanation.

The inside of the wire is metal. Metal is a good conductor and can easily move an electric current. People who touch wires having an electric current can get shocked. Plastic is an insulator and stops the flow of an electric current. People can hold the plastic-coated wires and not get shocked.

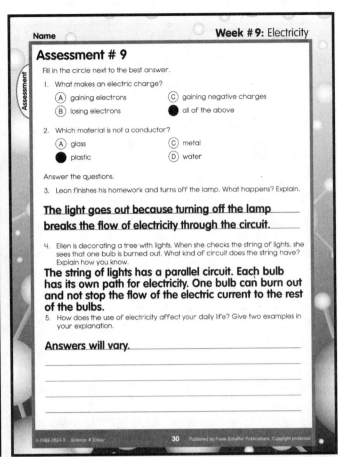

Assessment

Assessment # 9

Fill in the circle next to the best answer.

1. What makes an electric charge?
   - (A) gaining electrons
   - (B) losing electrons
   - (C) gaining negative charges
   - ● all of the above

2. Which material is not a conductor?
   - (A) glass
   - ● plastic
   - (C) metal
   - (D) water

Answer the questions.

3. Leon finishes his homework and turns off the lamp. What happens? Explain.

The light goes out because turning off the lamp breaks the flow of electricity through the circuit.

4. Ellen is decorating a tree with lights. When she checks the string of lights, she sees that one bulb is burned out. What kind of circuit does the string have? Explain how you know.

The string of lights has a parallel circuit. Each bulb has its own path for electricity. One bulb can burn out and not stop the flow of the electric current to the rest of the bulbs.

5. How does the use of electricity affect your daily life? Give two examples in your explanation.

Answers will vary.

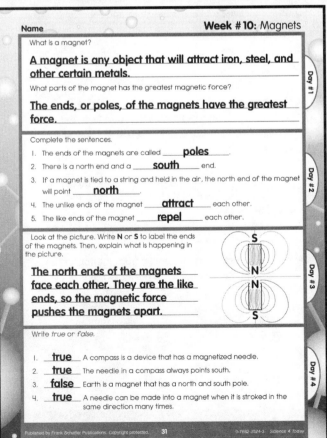

Day #1

What is a magnet?

A magnet is any object that will attract iron, steel, and other certain metals.

What parts of the magnet has the greatest magnetic force?

The ends, or poles, of the magnets have the greatest force.

Day #2

Complete the sentences.

1. The ends of the magnets are called **poles**.
2. There is a north end and a **south** end.
3. If a magnet is tied to a string and held in the air, the north end of the magnet will point **north**.
4. The unlike ends of the magnet **attract** each other.
5. The like ends of the magnet **repel** each other.

Day #3

Look at the picture. Write **N** or **S** to label the ends of the magnets. Then, explain what is happening in the picture.

S
N
N
S

The north ends of the magnets face each other. They are the like ends, so the magnetic force pushes the magnets apart.

Day #4

Write true or false.

1. **true** A compass is a device that has a magnetized needle.
2. **true** The needle in a compass always points south.
3. **false** Earth is a magnet that has a north and south pole.
4. **true** A needle can be made into a magnet when it is stroked in the same direction many times.

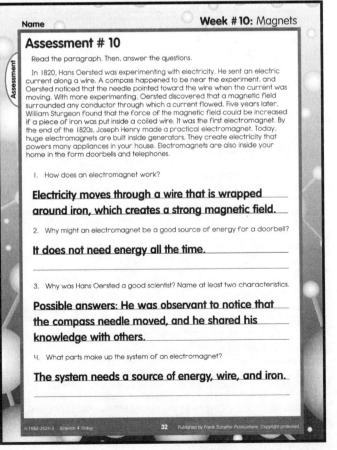

Assessment

Assessment # 10

Read the paragraph. Then, answer the questions.

In 1820, Hans Oersted was experimenting with electricity. He sent an electric current along a wire. A compass happened to be near the experiment, and Oersted noticed that the needle pointed toward the wire when the current was moving. With more experimenting, Oersted discovered that a magnetic field surrounded any conductor through which a current flowed. Five years later, William Sturgeon found that the force of the magnetic field could be increased if a piece of iron was put inside a coiled wire. It was the first electromagnet. By the end of the 1820s, Joseph Henry made a practical electromagnet. Today, huge electromagnets are built inside generators. They create electricity that powers many appliances in your house. Electromagnets are also inside your home in the form doorbells and telephones.

1. How does an electromagnet work?

Electricity moves through a wire that is wrapped around iron, which creates a strong magnetic field.

2. Why might an electromagnet be a good source of energy for a doorbell?

It does not need energy all the time.

3. Why was Hans Oersted a good scientist? Name at least two characteristics.

Possible answers: He was observant to notice that the compass needle moved, and he shared his knowledge with others.

4. What parts make up the system of an electromagnet?

The system needs a source of energy, wire, and iron.

Answer Key

Name   **Week # 11:** Sound

Listen to the sounds around you. Name three sounds that are made by natural objects and three sounds made by human-made objects.

Natural sounds: **Answers will vary.**

Human-made sounds: **Answers will vary.**

How are all sounds made? **All sounds are made when things vibrate.**

Day #1

What are sound waves?
Possible answer: Sound waves are the movement of molecules as they vibrate.
How do sound waves move?

Sounds waves move in a straight line. When the vibrations move through matter, they push close together. When they pass, they move farther apart.

Day #2

What is volume?

Volume is how loud or soft a sound is.

Why does shouting have more volume than whispering?

A shout is louder. A loud sound takes more energy to produce. The sound wave is bigger and travels farther.

Day #3

Circle the sound wave that has a low pitch.

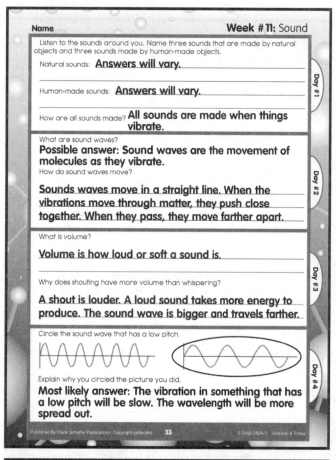

Explain why you circled the picture you did.
Most likely answer: The vibration in something that has a low pitch will be slow. The wavelength will be more spread out.

Day #4

Name   **Week # 11:** Sound

Assessment # 11

Look at the graph. Then, answer the questions.

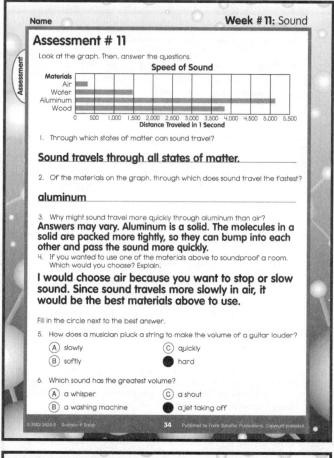

1. Through which states of matter can sound travel?

Sound travels through all states of matter.

2. Of the materials on the graph, through which does sound travel the fastest?

aluminum

3. Why might sound travel more quickly through aluminum than air?
Answers may vary. Aluminum is a solid. The molecules in a solid are packed more tightly, so they can bump into each other and pass the sound more quickly.

4. If you wanted to use one of the materials above to soundproof a room. Which would you choose? Explain.

I would choose air because you want to stop or slow sound. Since sound travels more slowly in air, it would be the best materials above to use.

Fill in the circle next to the best answer.

5. How does a musician pluck a string to make the volume of a guitar louder?
- (A) slowly
- (B) softly
- (C) quickly
- ● hard

6. Which sound has the greatest volume?
- (A) a whisper
- (B) a washing machine
- (C) a shout
- ● a jet taking off

Name   **Week # 12:** The Structure and Function of Plants

Write a **P** in front of each characteristic of a plant.

- **P** can grow
- **P** made of cells
- ___ needs shelter
- **P** makes its own food
- ___ learns behavior
- **P** can reproduce
- ___ gets foods from dead organisms
- **P** cannot move

Day #1

What are the two main groups of plants? Give two examples of each.

Group 1: **Answer order may vary. One group of plants makes seeds. Examples will vary.**
Group 2: **One group of plants does not make seeds. Examples will vary.**

Yes, a daisy and a pine tree belong in the same main group because both plants make seeds.

Day #2

Label the parts of a flower. Tell what each part does.

stamen- makes the pollen for fertilization

sepal- covers the flower buds

petal- keeps the parts that make seeds safe

pistil- makes the eggs that grow into seeds

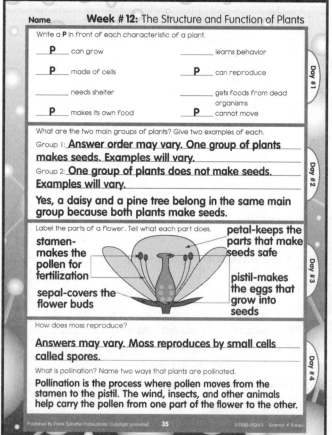

Day #3

How does moss reproduce?

Answers may vary. Moss reproduces by small cells called spores.

What is pollination? Name two ways that plants are pollinated.
Pollination is the process where pollen moves from the stamen to the pistil. The wind, insects, and other animals help carry the pollen from one part of the flower to the other.

Day #4

Name   **Week # 12:** The Structure and Function of Plants

Assessment # 12

Answer the questions.

1. Explain fertilization of a flowering plant. Use the words in the box in your explanation.

| pollen pistil | ovary | sperm | egg | seed |

Possible answer: After a flower is fertilized with pollen, each pollen grain grows a tube from the pistil down to the ovary. Sperm in the pollen joins with an egg in the ovary to make a seed.

2. How do insects pollinate flowers?

Insects visit the flowers to get nectar. The pollen sticks to their bodies. As they fly to other flowers, the pollen sticks to the pistils.

3. A corn plant grows two kinds of flowers. The flowers that have the stamens grow at the top of the stalk. The flowers that have the pistils grow on the rest of the stalk. How does the plant reproduce?

Wind or insects carry the pollen from the top of the plant to the flowers below to pollinate them.

Fill in the circle next to the best answer.

4. What is the name of the process where seeds begin to grow?
- (A) fertilization
- ● germination
- (C) pollination
- (D) classification

5. Which plant reproduces using spores?
- (A) oak tree
- (B) rose
- (C) grass
- ● fern

Answer Key

Unscramble the letters in bold to make words that tell about animal characteristics.

Day #1

1. reproduce
2. food
3. shelter
4. young
5. oxygen

Day #2

Answer order may vary.
Group 1: One group of animals has backbones.
 Examples will vary.
Group 2: One group of animals does not have backbones.
 Examples will vary.
Possible answer: They are alike because they do not have backbones. They are different because the beetle has an exoskeleton and jointed legs. The worm has a soft body and no legs.

Day #3

Animals with backbones can be classified into smaller groups, or classes. Draw a line to match each class with one of its characteristics.

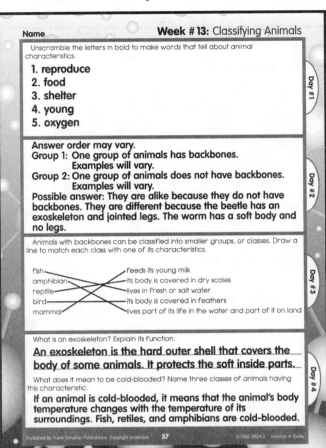

fish — feeds its young milk
amphibian — its body is covered in dry scales
reptile — lives in fresh or salt water
bird — its body is covered in feathers
mammal — lives part of its life in the water and part of it on land

Day #4

What is an exoskeleton? Explain its function.
An exoskeleton is the hard outer shell that covers the body of some animals. It protects the soft inside parts.

What does it mean to be cold-blooded? Name three classes of animals having this characteristic.
If an animal is cold-blooded, it means that the animal's body temperature changes with the temperature of its surroundings. Fish, retiles, and amphibians are cold-blooded.

Assessment # 13

Assessment

Answer the questions.

1. What is a backbone? Explain why it is an important characteristic to scientists who study animals.

The backbone is made up of many small bones and runs along the middle of the back in most animals. It supports the body. It is an important characteristic because scientists use it to classify animals into two main groups—those with backbones and those without.

2. Read the animal names in the box. Write each name in the correct class below.

hawk	whale	salamander	parrot	alligator
bass	shark	snake	human	frog

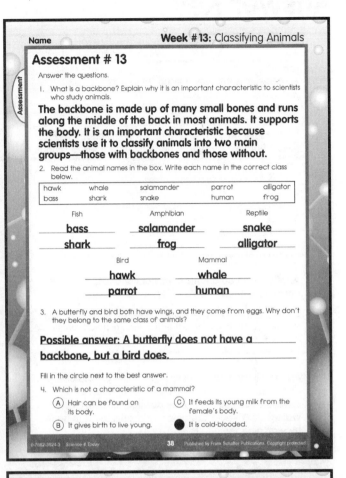

Fish	Amphibian	Reptile
bass	salamander	snake
shark	frog	alligator

Bird	Mammal
hawk	whale
parrot	human

3. A butterfly and bird both have wings, and they come from eggs. Why don't they belong to the same class of animals?

Possible answer: A butterfly does not have a backbone, but a bird does.

Fill in the circle next to the best answer.

4. Which is not a characteristic of a mammal?
 Ⓐ Hair can be found on its body.
 Ⓒ It feeds its young milk from the female's body.
 Ⓑ It gives birth to live young.
 ● It is cold-blooded.

Write a word from the box to complete each definition.

| trait | diversity | inherit | heredity | species |

Day #1

1. **heredity**— the passing of characteristics from one generation to the next
2. **diversity**— the condition of being different
3. **species**— a group of animals that can reproduce
4. **trait** — a feature or characteristic gotten from a parent
5. **inherit**— to get a characteristic from a parent or ancestor

Day #2

Possible answers: They may be stronger in one skill and have a better chance to survive. A species that is different is more interesting. Differences may mean that an animal will reproduce more and pass on those stronger traits.

Possible answers: Being different may make an animal more noticeable and cause it to be an easy prey. An animal that is different may not be accepted by the species and may be left to die.

Day #3

Why is it important that animals inherit traits from their parents?
Possible answer: They need to inherit traits so they can live survive in the habitat.

What are three specific traits that you inherited from your parents that your friends did not?
Answers will vary.

Day #4

A species can differ in several ways. Some animals have inherited a characteristic, but individual conditions affect its growth and development. For example, all the people in a family may be tall. The offspring will probably be tall, too. The body systems and the environment will affect just how tall, though. Think about other animals. What are two inherited characteristics that affect an organism? Explain.
Answers will vary.

Assessment # 14

Assessment

Answer the questions.

1. How does heredity affect a species?

Heredity makes sure that certain traits are passed down in a species so they can survive in the habitat.

2. What are three main differences in a species? Give an example of each.

There are specific traits inherited from a parent, such as eye color. There are inherited traits that are affected by the body systems and environment, such as height. There are acquired skills, like playing an instrument.

3. Do you think it is better to have diversity in a species or not? Explain.

Answers will vary.

Answer Key

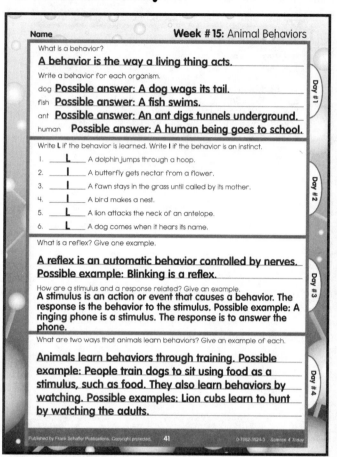

Name

Week # 15: Animal Behaviors

What is a behavior?

A behavior is the way a living thing acts.

Write a behavior for each organism.

dog **Possible answer: A dog wags its tail.**

fish **Possible answer: A fish swims.**

ant **Possible answer: An ant digs tunnels underground.**

human **Possible answer: A human being goes to school.**

Day #1

Write **L** if the behavior is learned. Write **I** if the behavior is an instinct.

1. **L** A dolphin jumps through a hoop.
2. **I** A butterfly gets nectar from a flower.
3. **I** A fawn stays in the grass until called by its mother.
4. **I** A bird makes a nest.
5. **L** A lion attacks the neck of an antelope.
6. **L** A dog comes when it hears its name.

Day #2

What is a reflex? Give one example.

A reflex is an automatic behavior controlled by nerves. Possible example: Blinking is a reflex.

How are a stimulus and a response related? Give an example.
A stimulus is an action or event that causes a behavior. The response is the behavior to the stimulus. Possible example: A ringing phone is a stimulus. The response is to answer the phone.

Day #3

What are two ways that animals learn behaviors? Give an example of each.

Animals learn behaviors through training. Possible example: People train dogs to sit using food as a stimulus, such as food. They also learn behaviors by watching. Possible examples: Lion cubs learn to hunt by watching the adults.

Day #4

Published by Frank Schaffer Publications. Copyright protected. **41**   0-7682-3524-3 *Science 4 Today*

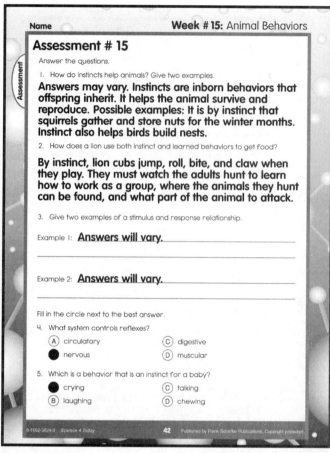

Assessment

Name

Week # 15: Animal Behaviors

Assessment # 15

Answer the questions.

1. How do instincts help animals? Give two examples.

Answers may vary. Instincts are inborn behaviors that offspring inherit. It helps the animal survive and reproduce. Possible examples: It is by instinct that squirrels gather and store nuts for the winter months. Instinct also helps birds build nests.

2. How does a lion use both instinct and learned behaviors to get food?

By instinct, lion cubs jump, roll, bite, and claw when they play. They must watch the adults hunt to learn how to work as a group, where the animals they hunt can be found, and what part of the animal to attack.

3. Give two examples of a stimulus and response relationship.

Example 1: **Answers will vary.**

Example 2: **Answers will vary.**

Fill in the circle next to the best answer.

4. What system controls reflexes?
   - Ⓐ circulatory
   - ● nervous
   - Ⓒ digestive
   - Ⓓ muscular

5. Which is a behavior that is an instinct for a baby?
   - ● crying
   - Ⓑ laughing
   - Ⓒ talking
   - Ⓓ chewing

0-7682-3524-3 *Science 4 Today* **42** Published by Frank Schaffer Publications. Copyright protected.

Name

Week # 16: Organisms and Energy

What is the process by which plants get food energy? Identify the three things plants need in the process.
Photosynthesis is the process. Plants need sunlight, water, and carbon dioxide in the process.
How does a plant use its leaves in the process?
Possible answer: Chlorophyll in the leaf traps light energy. Carbon dioxide is taken in through small holes on the underside of the plant. It mixes with light energy, water, and carbon dioxide to make sugar.

Day #1

Unscramble the letters in bold to make a word that completes each sentence.

1. energy
2. sugar
3. consumers
4. herbivore
5. carnivore
6. omnivore

Day #2

What are two ways that the energy stored in dead organisms is used? Give examples of each.
Some animals, like buzzards, eat the dead animals to get the energy. Decomposers, like worms and mushrooms, break down the bodies of dead organisms.
What is the relationship between decomposers and plants?
A decomposer returns the nutrients stored in dead organisms to the soil so that plants can use them.

Day #3

Write **1** through **6** to show how energy is passed along in a food chain.

- **4** spider
- **3** cricket
- **1** sun
- **6** snake
- **2** grass
- **5** frog

Day #4

Published by Frank Schaffer Publications. Copyright protected. **43**   0-7682-3524-3 *Science 4 Today*

Assessment

Name

Week # 16: Organisms and Energy

Assessment # 16

Answer the questions.

1. Give an example of a food chain that has at least four organisms.

Answers will vary.

2. Explain how human beings can harm the food chain you listed and its affects on the other living things.

Answers will vary.

3. What are some ways that human beings can help the food chain you listed?

Answers will vary.

Fill in the circle next to the best answer.

4. What is the main source of energy for plants?
   - ● sugar
   - Ⓑ nutrients
   - Ⓒ decomposers
   - Ⓓ oxygen

5. How is energy passed from one organism to another?
   - Ⓐ chlorophyll
   - ● food chains
   - Ⓒ photosynthesis
   - Ⓓ oxygen

0-7682-3524-3 *Science 4 Today* **44** Published by Frank Schaffer Publications. Copyright protected.

Answer Key

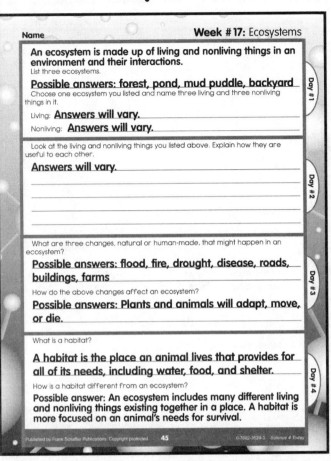

An ecosystem is made up of living and nonliving things in an environment and their interactions.
List three ecosystems.

Possible answers: forest, pond, mud puddle, backyard

Choose one ecosystem you listed and name three living and three nonliving things in it.

Living: **Answers will vary.**

Nonliving: **Answers will vary.**

Day #1

Look at the living and nonliving things you listed above. Explain how they are useful to each other.

Answers will vary.

Day #2

What are three changes, natural or human-made, that might happen in an ecosystem?

Possible answers: flood, fire, drought, disease, roads, buildings, farms

How do the above changes affect an ecosystem?

Possible answers: Plants and animals will adapt, move, or die.

Day #3

What is a habitat?

A habitat is the place an animal lives that provides for all of its needs, including water, food, and shelter.

How is a habitat different from an ecosystem?

Possible answer: An ecosystem includes many different living and nonliving things existing together in a place. A habitat is more focused on an animal's needs for survival.

Day #4

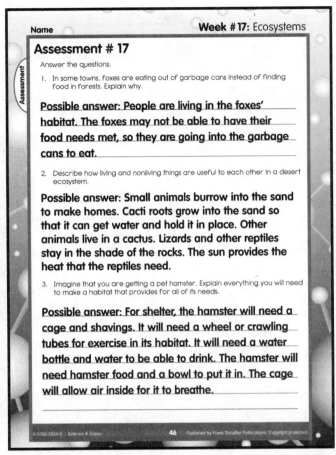

Assessment # 17

Answer the questions.

1. In some towns, foxes are eating out of garbage cans instead of finding food in forests. Explain why.

Possible answer: People are living in the foxes' habitat. The foxes may not be able to have their food needs met, so they are going into the garbage cans to eat.

2. Describe how living and nonliving things are useful to each other in a desert ecosystem.

Possible answer: Small animals burrow into the sand to make homes. Cacti roots grow into the sand so that it can get water and hold it in place. Other animals live in a cactus. Lizards and other reptiles stay in the shade of the rocks. The sun provides the heat that the reptiles need.

3. Imagine that you are getting a pet hamster. Explain everything you will need to make a habitat that provides for all of its needs.

Possible answer: For shelter, the hamster will need a cage and shavings. It will need a wheel or crawling tubes for exercise in its habitat. It will need a water bottle and water to be able to drink. The hamster will need hamster food and a bowl to put it in. The cage will allow air inside for it to breathe.

Assessment

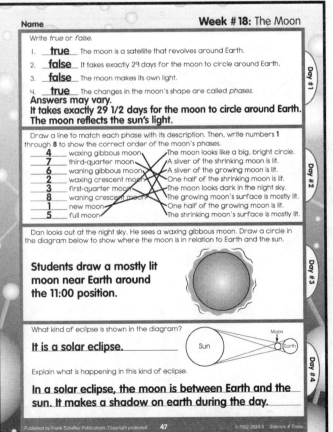

Write *true* or *false*.

1. **true** The moon is a satellite that revolves around Earth.
2. **false** It takes exactly 29 days for the moon to circle around Earth.
3. **false** The moon makes its own light.
4. **true** The changes in the moon's shape are called *phases*.

Answers may vary.
It takes exactly 29 1/2 days for the moon to circle around Earth.
The moon reflects the sun's light.

Day #1

Draw a line to match each phase with its description. Then, write numbers **1** through **8** to show the correct order of the moon's phases.

4	waxing gibbous moon	The moon looks like a big, bright circle.
7	third-quarter moon	A sliver of the shrinking moon is lit.
6	waning gibbous moon	A sliver of the growing moon is lit.
2	waxing crescent moon	One half of the shrinking moon is lit.
3	first-quarter moon	The moon looks dark in the night sky.
8	waning crescent moon	The growing moon's surface is mostly lit.
1	new moon	One half of the growing moon is lit.
5	full moon	The shrinking moon's surface is mostly lit.

Day #2

Dan looks out at the night sky. He sees a waxing gibbous moon. Draw a circle in the diagram below to show where the moon is in relation to Earth and the sun.

Students draw a mostly lit moon near Earth around the 11:00 position.

Day #3

What kind of eclipse is shown in the diagram?

It is a solar eclipse.

Explain what is happening in this kind of eclipse.

In a solar eclipse, the moon is between Earth and the sun. It makes a shadow on earth during the day.

Day #4

Assessment # 18

Answer the questions.

1. What is the difference in a solar and lunar eclipse?

Possible answer: In a solar eclipse, the moon is between the Earth and the sun and makes a shadow on Earth in the daytime. In a lunar eclipse, the Earth is between the sun and moon, and the Earth's shadow darkens the moon at night.

2. What is a new moon? Explain what it looks like and why it has this appearance.

The new moon is the beginning of the phases of the moon. The dark half faces Earth, so it cannot be seen.

3. What is the difference in a waning crescent and waxing crescent moon?

The waning crescent moon means the moon is near the end of its cycle, and only a sliver of its surface is lit. The waxing crescent means the moon is beginning its cycle, and only a sliver of its surface is lit.

4. Depak sees the moon shown below. What is the name of the moon he sees? Which phase of the moon will he see several nights later?

Depak sees a third-quarter moon. He will see a waning crescent moon next.

5. Which phase of the moon is your nighttime sky now? Explain how you know.

Answers will vary.

Assessment

Answer Key

Day #1

Label the four layers of Earth. Write one fact about each layer.

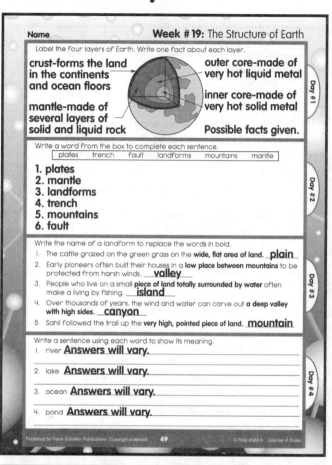

crust-forms the land in the continents and ocean floors

mantle-made of several layers of solid and liquid rock

outer core-made of very hot liquid metal

inner core-made of very hot solid metal

Possible facts given.

Day #2

Write a word from the box to complete each sentence.

| plates | trench | fault | landforms | mountains | mantle |

1. plates
2. mantle
3. landforms
4. trench
5. mountains
6. fault

Day #3

Write the name of a landform to replace the words in bold.

1. The cattle grazed on the green grass on the **wide, flat area of land.** __plain__
2. Early pioneers often built their houses in a **low place between mountains** to be protected from harsh winds. __valley__
3. People who live on a small **piece of land totally surrounded by water** often make a living by fishing. __island__
4. Over thousands of years, the wind and water can carve out **a deep valley with high sides.** __canyon__
5. Sahil followed the trail up the **very high, pointed piece of land.** __mountain__

Day #4

Write a sentence using each word to show its meaning.

1. river __Answers will vary.__
2. lake __Answers will vary.__
3. ocean __Answers will vary.__
4. pond __Answers will vary.__

Assessment

Assessment # 19

Fill in the circle next to the best answer.

1. Which layer of Earth is no thicker than 20 miles?
   - Ⓐ inner core
   - Ⓑ outer core
   - Ⓒ mantle
   - ● crust

2. Where do most earthquakes occur?
   - ● at a fault
   - Ⓑ in a trench
   - Ⓒ on top of a mountain
   - Ⓓ near a lake

Answer the questions.

3. How do plates move? Describe how the movement affects Earth's surface.

Possible answer: Plates move away from, toward, and past each other. Where the plates meet is where changes occur. If they collide, one plate may slide under another to form trenches and mountains. If the slide past each other, they form a fault.

4. Which landforms or water features are nearby? Describe the characteristics of the places to identify them.

Answers will vary.

Day #1

What is a mineral?

__A mineral is nonliving solid matter found in nature.__

Write **P** in front of the properties that help scientist classify minerals.

__P__	how hard it is	__P__	its color
__P__	how shiny it is	___	its temperature
__P__	how it breaks	__P__	if it is magnetic
___	how it smells	___	its size

Day #2

What are the three kinds of rocks? Tell how each is formed?
Answer order may vary.
Category 1: Sedimentary rocks form when many layers of sediment pile on top of each other. They are pressed together and harden.
Category 2: Igneous rocks form when hot, liquid rock cools and hardens.
Category 3: Metamorphic rock is made from sedimentary or igneous rock that has been heated and pressed together.

Day #3

Circle the word that best completes each sentence.

1. A (fossil) rock) is the remains or mark left behind by a living thing that died long ago.
2. These kinds of remains are often found in (metamorphic, (sedimentary)) rocks.
3. The ((imprint) cast) shows the mold of something thin, like a wing or leaf.
4. Some fuels we use today, like (ore, (coal)), are actually fossils formed from plants that lived long ago.

Day #4

What is soil made of?

__Soil is made of tiny rocks (minerals), air, water, and humus (dead plants and animals).__

Possible answer: Over thousands of years, rocks are weathered by water, wind, plants, and ice, which break them into tiny pieces. Decomposers eat dead plants and animals, and their waste, full of nutrients and energy, mixes with the weathered rocks.

Assessment

Assessment # 20

Answer the questions.

1. Explain the four ways that rocks are weathered to form soil.

Rocks are weathered by water, wind, ice, and plants. The flow of water chips off tiny grains and pieces. Wind carries pieces of sand that hit bigger rocks, causing them to chip. Water also gets in cracks and freezes. As the ice expands, it forces the cracks to grow and can break the rock. Plant roots grow in the cracks of rocks. As they get bigger, they break the rocks.

2. Why is soil important?

Possible answer: Soil grows plants, which is the primary source of food for many animals. Plants also provide the air animals need to breathe.

3. What kind of soil do farmers look for when choosing where to plant crops? Explain.

__Farmers want soil rich in humus. The humus has lots of nutrients that plants need for healthy growth.__

Fill in the circle next to the best answer.

4. Which kind of soil is made by decomposers?
   - Ⓐ clay
   - ● humus
   - Ⓑ minerals
   - Ⓓ silt

5. Tran picks up a rock that easily breaks in his hands. What kind of rock is it?
   - ● sedimentary
   - Ⓒ metamorphic
   - Ⓑ volcanic
   - Ⓓ igneous

Answer Key

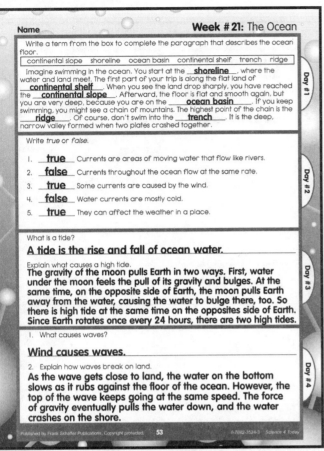

Write a term from the box to complete the paragraph that describes the ocean floor.

continental slope   shoreline   ocean basin   continental shelf   trench   ridge

Imagine swimming in the ocean. You start at the **shoreline**, where the water and land meet. The first part of your trip is along the flat land of **continental shelf**. When you see the land drop sharply, you have reached the **continental slope**. Afterward, the floor is flat and smooth again, but you are very deep, because you are on the **ocean basin**. If you keep swimming, you might see a chain of mountains. The highest point of the chain is the **ridge**. Of course, don't swim into the **trench**. It is the deep, narrow valley formed when two plates crashed together.

Day #1

Write *true* or *false*.

1. **true** Currents are areas of moving water that flow like rivers.
2. **false** Currents throughout the ocean flow at the same rate.
3. **true** Some currents are caused by the wind.
4. **false** Water currents are mostly cold.
5. **true** They can affect the weather in a place.

Day #2

What is a tide?

A tide is the rise and fall of ocean water.

Explain what causes a high tide.

The gravity of the moon pulls Earth in two ways. First, water under the moon feels the pull of its gravity and bulges. At the same time, on the opposite side of Earth, the moon pulls Earth away from the water, causing the water to bulge there, too. So there is high tide at the same time on the opposites side of Earth. Since Earth rotates once every 24 hours, there are two high tides.

Day #3

1. What causes waves?

Wind causes waves.

2. Explain how waves break on land.

As the wave gets close to land, the water on the bottom slows as it rubs against the floor of the ocean. However, the top of the wave keeps going at the same speed. The force of gravity eventually pulls the water down, and the water crashes on the shore.

Day #4

Assessment

Assessment # 21

Answer the questions.

1. How is the ocean a system? Give three examples of three living and nonliving things in it.

Answer will vary.

2. Choose one cycle in the ocean and describe it.

Answer will vary.

3. How is an ocean like a river? How is it different? Give two examples of each.

Possible answer: The ocean is like a river because it is a water feature filled with many living things. Currents in the ocean flow like a river. It is different because an ocean has salt water, while a river has fresh water. Oceans are much bigger than rivers, too.

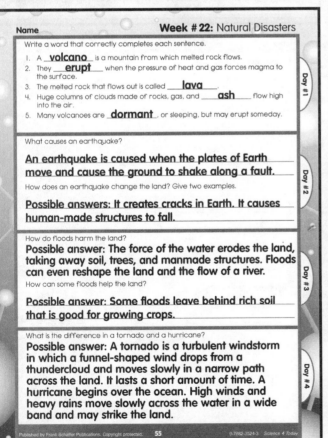

Write a word that correctly completes each sentence.

1. A **volcano** is a mountain from which melted rock flows.
2. They **erupt** when the pressure of heat and gas forces magma to the surface.
3. The melted rock that flows out is called **lava**.
4. Huge columns of clouds made of rocks, gas, and **ash** flow high into the air.
5. Many volcanoes are **dormant**, or sleeping, but may erupt someday.

Day #1

What causes an earthquake?

An earthquake is caused when the plates of Earth move and cause the ground to shake along a fault.

How does an earthquake change the land? Give two examples.

Possible answers: It creates cracks in Earth. It causes human-made structures to fall.

Day #2

How do floods harm the land?

Possible answer: The force of the water erodes the land, taking away soil, trees, and manmade structures. Floods can even reshape the land and the flow of a river.

How can some floods help the land?

Possible answer: Some floods leave behind rich soil that is good for growing crops.

Day #3

What is the difference in a tornado and a hurricane?

Possible answer: A tornado is a turbulent windstorm in which a funnel-shaped wind drops from a thundercloud and moves slowly in a narrow path across the land. It lasts a short amount of time. A hurricane begins over the ocean. High winds and heavy rains move slowly across the water in a wide band and may strike the land.

Day #4

Assessment

Assessment # 22

Answer the questions.

1. Will Earth look the same 100 years from now? Explain.

No, the land will be different due to changes made by events caused in nature.

2. Scientists have many devices to track the shaking of the ground around a fault line. Why would they do this?

Possible answer: If they see clues that an earthquake might happen, they can warn people and save lives.

3. Which is easier to predict—a tornado or a hurricane? Explain.

Possible answer: A hurricane is easier to predict since forecasters can track the movement for a long time before it strikes land. A tornado happens in thunderstorm conditions, which can appear instantly.

4. Volcanoes formed the Hawaiian Islands long ago. In fact, lava still flows out of some volcanoes today. Scientists also watch underwater volcanoes that are erupting. What do they predict will happen to Hawaii a thousand of years from now?

Most likely answer: Hawaii will get bigger because the lava is spreading out and forming new land.

Answer Key

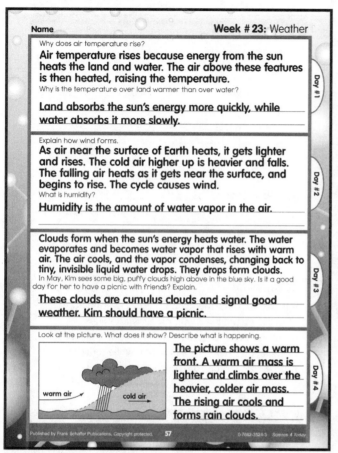

Name   **Week # 23:** Weather

Day #1

Why does air temperature rise?

Air temperature rises because energy from the sun heats the land and water. The air above these features is then heated, raising the temperature.

Why is the temperature over land warmer than over water?

Land absorbs the sun's energy more quickly, while water absorbs it more slowly.

Day #2

Explain how wind forms.

As air near the surface of Earth heats, it gets lighter and rises. The cold air higher up is heavier and falls. The falling air heats as it gets near the surface, and begins to rise. The cycle causes wind.

What is humidity?

Humidity is the amount of water vapor in the air.

Day #3

Clouds form when the sun's energy heats water. The water evaporates and becomes water vapor that rises with warm air. The air cools, and the vapor condenses, changing back to tiny, invisible liquid water drops. They drops form clouds.

In May, Kim sees some big, puffy clouds high above in the blue sky. Is it a good day for her to have a picnic with friends? Explain.

These clouds are cumulus clouds and signal good weather. Kim should have a picnic.

Day #4

Look at the picture. What does it show? Describe what is happening.

warm air   cold air

The picture shows a warm front. A warm air mass is lighter and climbs over the heavier, colder air mass. The rising air cools and forms rain clouds.

Published by Frank Schaffer Publications. Copyright protected.   **57**   0-7682-3524-3   Science 4 Today

---

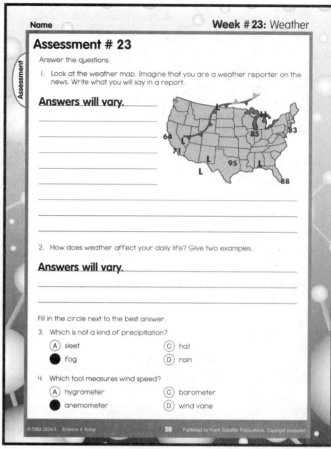

Name   **Week # 23:** Weather

Assessment

Assessment # 23

Answer the questions.

1. Look at the weather map. Imagine that you are a weather reporter on the news. Write what you will say in a report.

Answers will vary.

2. How does weather affect your daily life? Give two examples.

Answers will vary.

Fill in the circle next to the best answer.

3. Which is not a kind of precipitation?
   - (A) sleet
   - ● fog
   - (C) hail
   - (D) rain

4. Which tool measures wind speed?
   - (A) hygrometer
   - ● anemometer
   - (C) barometer
   - (D) wind vane

0-7682-3524-3   Science 4 Today   **58**   Published by Frank Schaffer Publications. Copyright protected.

Name   **Week # 24:** Amazing Human-made Modern Marvels

Day #1

In 1998, Japan built the Akashi Kaiko Bridge, the longest suspension bridge. It stretches more than 12,800 feet across a busy shipping port. High winds and earthquakes frequently occur in Japan, so engineers designed the bridge with these problems in mind. The two towers, reaching nearly 930 feet into the air, have open areas so the wind will blow through. Other parts sway to balance any movement in the bridge.

Possible answer: Since there is nothing for the wind to press on, the force will be smaller, so less damage will occur.

Day #2

Tall buildings have been around for centuries. Many were made of thick rock walls to support the weight. Using a steel skeleton made it possible to build tall skyscrapers. Until 2004, the two Petronas Towers in Malaysia were the tallest buildings in the world. Each are 1483 feet tall, including the spire, a tall, pointed decoration. The buildings have 88 stories.

Why might steel be a better building material than rock?

Possible answer: Steel is lighter, but can still support heavy weight. It can be shaped, too.

Day #3

There are tunnels everywhere under the ground. Workers build these tunnels to carry water, people, transportation, and wires. However, an engineer must carefully plan the construction. The ground must be examined and tested for the kind of rock and soil in the area. It is a slow process as workers must brace the ground above them as they dig.

Sedimentary rock would be the most unsafe, because it is a soft rock that would break easily. It would need much more support than metamorphic or igneous rocks.

Day #4

Dams are the largest structures that people build. They control flooding, watering crops, and electricity. Dams are also popular places for boating, swimming, and fishing. China is in the process of building the biggest dam. When complete, the Three Gorges Dam will be 1.4 miles wide and 630 feet high. The reservoir, or lake behind it, will be about 350 miles long, allowing large ships to travel to cities far inside the country. However, there are some problems with the dam. Millions of people have been forced off their farmland and ancient temples have been flooded.

If there were no dams, what might the world be like?

Answers will vary.

Published by Frank Schaffer Publications. Copyright protected.   **59**   0-7682-3524-3   Science 4 Today

---

Name   **Week # 24:** Amazing Human-made Modern Marvels

Assessment

Assessment # 24

Answer the questions.

1. The Sears Tower, located in the United States, is about 1,450 feet. It has two television antennae that, when added to the rooftop height, make the total structure 1,729 feet tall. People work on a floor that is actually 200 feet higher than the Petronas Towers. Yet building experts still claim that the Petronas Towers are taller because the spire is part of the building design. Do you agree that the Petronas Towers are taller than the Sears tower? Explain.

Answers will vary.

2. How do people benefit from manmade structures? Are they always helpful? Explain.

Answers will vary.

0-7682-3524-3   Science 4 Today   **60**   Published by Frank Schaffer Publications. Copyright protected.

Answer Key

Name   **Week #25:** Transportation

Day #1

How would you like to travel over 300 miles per hour—on land? In some countries, people are traveling this fast on maglev trains. While the cars look like those on a train, the maglev train uses electromagnets to move. The guideways that direct the train are lined with metal coils. As electricity moves along the guideways, large magnets on the underside of the car repel the magnetized coil. As a result, the train rises almost four inches above the track and glides forward.

The two like poles are facing each other because like poles repel each other. When they repel, they push away. The maglev rises into the air and moves as a result.

Day #2

Most cars on the road use gasoline or diesel fuel. Both materials are fossil fuels and in limited supply. They are expensive, too. As a result, more and more people are driving hybrid cars. Hybrid cars use both an electric motor and gasoline engine for power. The electric motor starts the engine and gets it moving when the greatest amount of power is needed. The gasoline engine takes over when the cruising speed is reached. Less energy is needed when the car is in motion.

There is a lot of stopping and starting for lights in a city. Since the hybrid car uses electricity for starting and increasing speed, it would use less gasoline.

Day #3

Scientists are researching another power source for transportation—the sun. Energy from the sun is inexhaustible and will not run out. So scientists are experimenting with placing dark solar panels on lightweight vehicles. The panels absorb the sun's light, where it is changed into electric energy. The electric energy immediately powers the wheels or remains stored in a battery for a short time. While many scientists don't think a solar car will ever be practical, they are learning much about energy.

The cars would not work on cloudy days or at night when the sun does not shine.

Day #4

Corn is a source of energy for people and animals. It is also a source of energy for some vehicles. This renewable resource is being turned into a liquid fuel by removing the starch and turning it into sugar. Known as *ethanol*, this bio-fuel burns much more cleanly and reduces the pollution in the air. It can be used in both light vehicles and heavy trucks.

Possible answers: It is a renewable resource, meaning that it can be used and more can be grown. It does not produce fumes that pollute.

Name   **Week #25:** Transportation

Assessment

Assessment # 25

Answer the questions.

1. How might the maglev train both help and harm the environment?

Most trains use fossil fuels as the main source of power. They pollute the air with their fumes. Since maglev trains use electromagnets, there would be no air pollution directly rising from the train. However, maglev trains use electricity as a power source, which still comes from fossil fuels. So they are indirectly using a limited resource.

2. Name two reasons telling why people buy hybrid cars.

Answers will vary. _____

_____

_____

3. What are two important reasons that scientists are working to develop new forms of transportation?

Fossil fuels are running out, so people will need a way to power their vehicles once the resources are gone. Many vehicles that use fossil fumes produce smoke, which pollutes the air.

Fill in the circle next to the best answer.

4. Which vehicle does not use electricity?
   - (A) maglev train
   - (C) hybrid car
   - ● diesel train
   - (D) solar car

5. When does a hybrid use gasoline?
   - (A) when it starts
   - ● when it moves at a steady speed
   - (B) when it begins to speed
   - (D) when it stops

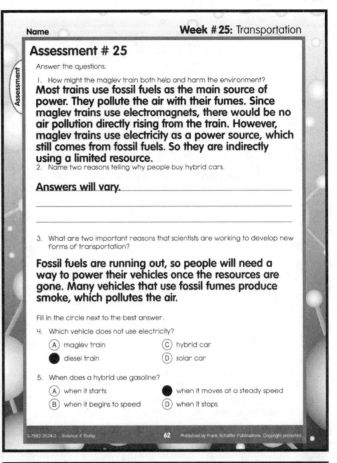

Name   **Week #26:** Ocean Technology

Day #1

The ocean is very deep. In some places, it is nearly 10,000 feet down to the floor. Pressure from the weight of the water, cold temperatures, and the lack of sunlight make it a dangerous place to visit. So how do scientist know so much about this ecosystem? They use *Alvin*. *Alvin* is the first ocean-diving vehicle that can carry several people to the bottom of the ocean. One dive especially surprised the scientists. They didn't think anything could live in the deep water. Yet, they saw tube worms and other amazing fish.

Why might scientists not expect to find living things in deep ocean water?

Answers will vary.

Day #2

NR-1 is a nuclear submarine that can dive in deep ocean water. It can stay there for up to a month, too. *NR-1* has mapped the ocean floor and looked for sunken ships using sonar. The ship sends out sound waves and waits for them to come back. Scientists can tell how deep something is by the time that it takes for the sound to return. *NR-1* even has a tool that can grip objects up to 2,000 pounds and pull them into the ship.

The floor below is not very deep. When a sound returns quickly, it means that the sound wave hit something that was close.

Day #3

Jason is a robot that explores the ocean floor. Because it is a robot, no one gets inside. *Jason* has cables that link it to computers on a ship. Scientists send information to *Jason* telling it where to go and what to videotape. *Jason* also has an arm that collects things that scientist want to see.

Possible answer: Both Jason and NR-1 are devices that explore the ocean. Both have an arm to pick up material and return it to the surface for scientists to study. They are different in that Jason is a robot and does not carry a crew.

Day #4

Possible answer: Both space and water environments are different from the ones support human life. Scientists have taken what they learned during space travel and used the info to help people explore the ocean.

Name   **Week #26:** Ocean Technology

Assessment

Assessment # 26

Answer the questions.

1. Why is ocean research important? Give three reasons.

Answers will vary. _____

_____

_____

_____

_____

_____

_____

2. Why is sonar a good tool to use in the ocean?

The ocean floor is dark, so scientists cannot see the bottom to map it. The sound waves help them know depths by how fast the waves bounce back.

3. Why might robots be more useful in ocean exploration? Give two reasons.

Possible answers: Robots can dive deeper without endangering people. Robots can fit into smaller spaces.

Answer Key

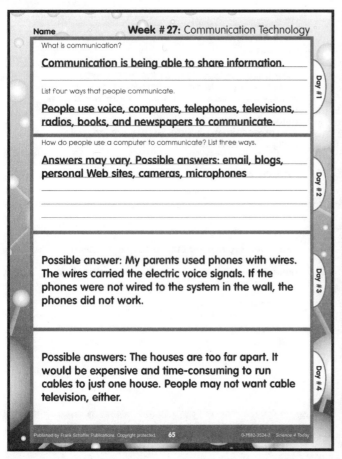

Name

Week # 27: Communication Technology

Day #1

What is communication?

Communication is being able to share information.

List four ways that people communicate.

People use voice, computers, telephones, televisions, radios, books, and newspapers to communicate.

Day #2

How do people use a computer to communicate? List three ways.

Answers may vary. Possible answers: email, blogs, personal Web sites, cameras, microphones

Day #3

Possible answer: My parents used phones with wires. The wires carried the electric voice signals. If the phones were not wired to the system in the wall, the phones did not work.

Day #4

Possible answers: The houses are too far apart. It would be expensive and time-consuming to run cables to just one house. People may not want cable television, either.

Name   **Week # 27:** Communication Technology

Assessment

Assessment # 27

Answer the questions.

1. How has technology changed communication in the last 100 years?

Answers will vary.

2. List three ways that you use technology to communicate.

Answers will vary.

Name   **Week # 28:** Robot Technology

Day #1

A robot is a device that gathers information about the environment and reacts to the information almost immediately. They are usually designed for a specific task. They may have cameras that act as eyes and sensors that pick up sound waves to hear. Scientists load information into a computer system that helps these devices work.

How is a robot like a machine? How are they different?

Possible answer: Both have moving parts and do a job. A robot has a computer that helps it gather information and allows it to react to the environment.

Day #2

Name two robots that you use. Tell why they are robots.

Answers will vary.

Why do people build robots?

People build robots to do a job or to entertain.

Day #3

Many factories use robots. Most robots are computers with arms that do a single task. What are two reasons that robots are a good choice for working in factories?

Possible answers: Robots can work nonstop without getting tired. They do repetitive tasks that are boring to workers. They are cheaper to operate, and they are safer.

Day #4

Two robots were sent to Mars to explore its surface. The robots, called *rovers*, were autonomous, meaning that they reacted to things they found in the environment without direction from people. The robots rolled on the surface of Mars and took pictures. Arms could hold different tools to take samples of the soil and rocks. The information and pictures were sent to scientists on Earth.

Where else could robots be used?

Answers will vary.

Name   **Week # 28:** Robot Technology

Assessment

Assessment # 28

Answer the questions.

1. Robots often do tasks that people do not want to do. If you could design a robot, what task would you have it do? How might this affect you and your life?

Answers will vary.

2. What are two reasons that robots might be harmful to society?

Possible answers: They are doing more jobs in factories, which means that people are losing jobs. They are doing more daily tasks, so people are getting lazy.

Answer Key

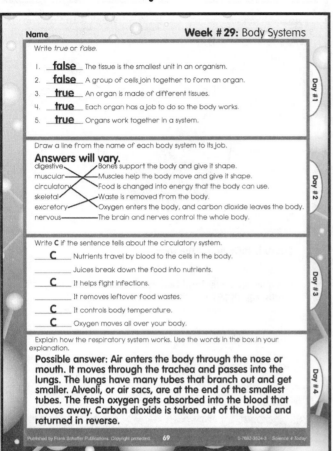

Name | **Week #29:** Body Systems

Write *true* or *false*.

1. **false** The tissue is the smallest unit in an organism.
2. **false** A group of cells join together to form an organ.
3. **true** An organ is made of different tissues.
4. **true** Each organ has a job to do so the body works.
5. **true** Organs work together in a system.

Day #1

Draw a line from the name of each body system to its job.

Answers will vary.

digestive — Bones support the body and give it shape.
muscular — Muscles help the body move and give it shape.
circulatory — Food is changed into energy that the body can use.
skeletal — Waste is removed from the body.
excretory — Oxygen enters the body, and carbon dioxide leaves the body.
nervous — The brain and nerves control the whole body.

Day #2

Write **C** if the sentence tells about the circulatory system.

C Nutrients travel by blood to the cells in the body.
___ Juices break down the food into nutrients.
C It helps fight infections.
___ It removes leftover food wastes.
C It controls body temperature.
C Oxygen moves all over your body.

Day #3

Explain how the respiratory system works. Use the words in the box in your explanation.

Possible answer: Air enters the body through the nose or mouth. It moves through the trachea and passes into the lungs. The lungs have many tubes that branch out and get smaller. Alveoli, or air sacs, are at the end of the smallest tubes. The fresh oxygen gets absorbed into the blood that moves away. Carbon dioxide is taken out of the blood and returned in reverse.

Day #4

Published by Frank Schaffer Publications. Copyright protected. 69   0-7682-3524-3   *Science 4 Today*

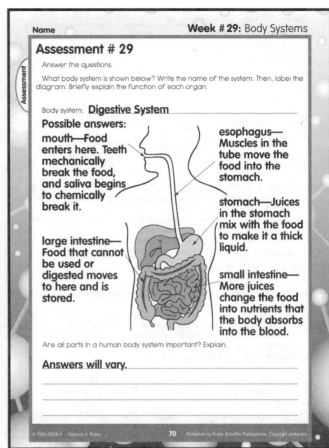

Name | **Week #29:** Body Systems

Assessment #29

Assessment

Answer the questions.

What body system is shown below? Write the name of the system. Then, label the diagram. Briefly explain the function of each organ.

Body system: **Digestive System**

Possible answers:

mouth—Food enters here. Teeth mechanically break the food, and saliva begins to chemically break it.

esophagus— Muscles in the tube move the food into the stomach.

stomach—Juices in the stomach mix with the food to make it a thick liquid.

large intestine— Food that cannot be used or digested moves to here and is stored.

small intestine— More juices change the food into nutrients that the body absorbs into the blood.

Are all parts in a human body system important? Explain.

Answers will vary. _____

0-7682-3524-3   *Science 4 Today*   70   Published by Frank Schaffer Publications. Copyright protected.

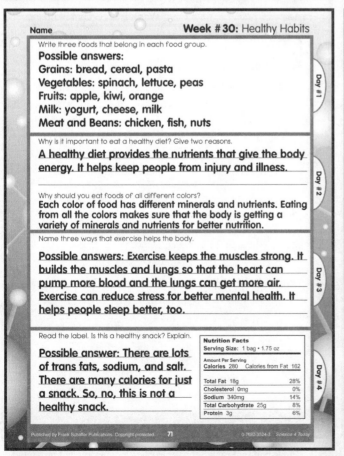

Name | **Week #30:** Healthy Habits

Write three foods that belong in each food group.

Possible answers:
Grains: bread, cereal, pasta
Vegetables: spinach, lettuce, peas
Fruits: apple, kiwi, orange
Milk: yogurt, cheese, milk
Meat and Beans: chicken, fish, nuts

Day #1

Why is it important to eat a healthy diet? Give two reasons.

A healthy diet provides the nutrients that give the body energy. It helps keep people from injury and illness.

Day #2

Why should you eat foods of all different colors?
Each color of food has different minerals and nutrients. Eating from all the colors makes sure that the body is getting a variety of minerals and nutrients for better nutrition.

Name three ways that exercise helps the body.

Possible answers: Exercise keeps the muscles strong. It builds the muscles and lungs so that the heart can pump more blood and the lungs can get more air. Exercise can reduce stress for better mental health. It helps people sleep better, too.

Day #3

Read the label. Is this a healthy snack? Explain.

Possible answer: There are lots of trans fats, sodium, and salt. There are many calories for just a snack. So, no, this is not a healthy snack.

Nutrition Facts
Serving Size: 1 bag • 1.75 oz

Amount Per Serving
Calories 280   Calories from Fat 162

Total Fat 18g	28%
Cholesterol 0mg	0%
Sodium 340mg	14%
Total Carbohydrate 25g	8%
Protein 3g	6%

Day #4

Published by Frank Schaffer Publications. Copyright protected. 71   0-7682-3524-3   *Science 4 Today*

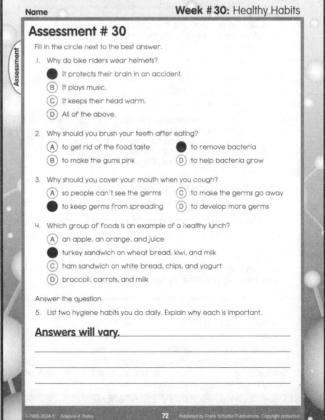

Name | **Week #30:** Healthy Habits

Assessment #30

Assessment

Fill in the circle next to the best answer.

1. Why do bike riders wear helmets?
   - ● It protects their brain in an accident.
   - Ⓑ It plays music.
   - Ⓒ It keeps their head warm.
   - Ⓓ All of the above.

2. Why should you brush your teeth after eating?
   - Ⓐ to get rid of the food taste
   - ● to remove bacteria
   - Ⓑ to make the gums pink
   - Ⓓ to help bacteria grow

3. Why should you cover your mouth when you cough?
   - Ⓐ so people can't see the germs
   - Ⓒ to make the germs go away
   - ● to keep germs from spreading
   - Ⓓ to develop more germs

4. Which group of foods is an example of a healthy lunch?
   - Ⓐ an apple, an orange, and juice
   - ● turkey sandwich on wheat bread, kiwi, and milk
   - Ⓒ ham sandwich on white bread, chips, and yogurt
   - Ⓓ broccoli, carrots, and milk

Answer the question.

5. List two hygiene habits you do daily. Explain why each is important.

Answers will vary. _____

0-7682-3524-3   *Science 4 Today*   72   Published by Frank Schaffer Publications. Copyright protected.

Answer Key

Name

Week # 31: Pollution

Write a word to correctly complete each sentence.

1. pollution
2. land
3. noise
4. water
5. air
6. light

Day #1

List three causes of air pollution.

Possible answers: Car fumes, coal-burning electric plants, forest fires, and volcanoes cause air pollution.

Possible answer: Ash and dust cover the leaves making it difficult for the plants to get the sunlight energy they need for photosynthesis.

Day #2

List three causes of water pollution.

Possible answers: Leaking oil tankers leak, leaking sewage plants, boat fumes, and trash people toss into the water cause water pollution.

How does water pollution affect animals?

Possible answer: Animals get sick when they drink the water.

Day #3

Possible answer: There may be chemicals in the landfill, which run off onto the nearby farmland. The poison kills the crops or is absorbed into the plants, making people and animals that eat them sick.

What is one way that communities reuse landfills? How does this help the community?

Possible answer: People cover up the landfill and build parks and office buildings on top, making the land useful again.

Day #4

73   0-7682-3524-3   Science 4 Today

Name

Week # 31: Pollution

Assessment

Assessment # 31

Look at the graph. Then, answer the questions.

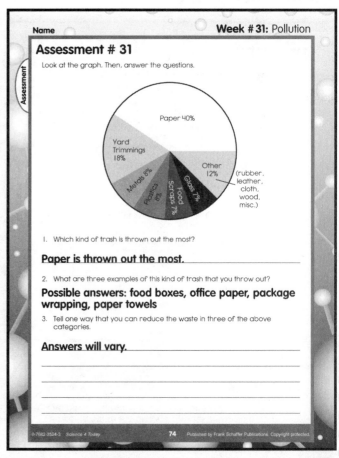

Paper 40%
Yard Trimmings 18%
Other 12% (rubber, leather, cloth, wood, misc.)
Metals 8%
Plastics 8%
Food Scraps 7%
Glass 7%

1. Which kind of trash is thrown out the most?

Paper is thrown out the most.

2. What are three examples of this kind of trash that you throw out?

Possible answers: food boxes, office paper, package wrapping, paper towels

3. Tell one way that you can reduce the waste in three of the above categories.

Answers will vary.

0-7682-3524-3   Science 4 Today   74   Published by Frank Schaffer Publications. Copyright protected.

Name

Week # 32: Global Warming

What is the greenhouse effect?

The greenhouse effect is the process in which the blanket of air around Earth traps some of the sun's rays and heats the land.

Why is this system important to Earth?

It is important because it heats Earth, making it warm enough for organisms to live.

Day #1

What does the picture show?

The picture shows that some of the sun's heat is reflected off the ground. It strikes the heavy layer of gases and reflects back to earth instead of escaping into space. Earth absorbs the heat this time.

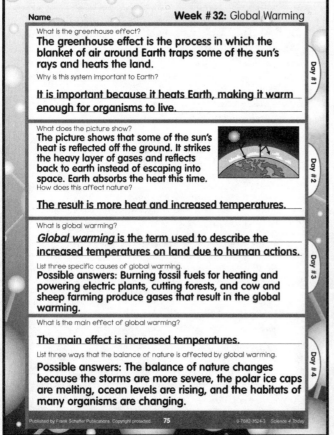

How does this affect nature?

The result is more heat and increased temperatures.

Day #2

What is global warming?

***Global warming* is the term used to describe the increased temperatures on land due to human actions.**

List three specific causes of global warming.

Possible answers: Burning fossil fuels for heating and powering electric plants, cutting forests, and cow and sheep farming produce gases that result in the global warming.

What is the main effect of global warming?

The main effect is increased temperatures.

List three ways that the balance of nature is affected by global warming.

Possible answers: The balance of nature changes because the storms are more severe, the polar ice caps are melting, ocean levels are rising, and the habitats of many organisms are changing.

Day #3

Day #4

Published by Frank Schaffer Publications. Copyright protected.   75   0-7682-3524-3   Science 4 Today

---

Name

Week # 32: Global Warming

Assessment

Assessment # 32

Answer the questions.

1. How does the greenhouse effect affect the balance of nature?

Answers will vary.

2. What are three things that you can do to reduce global warming?

Answers will vary.

0-7682-3524-3   Science 4 Today   76   Published by Frank Schaffer Publications. Copyright protected.

Answer Key

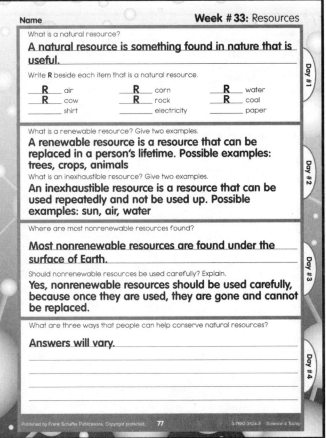

What is a natural resource?

A natural resource is something found in nature that is useful.

Write **R** beside each item that is a natural resource.

R	air	**R**	corn	**R**	water
R	cow	**R**	rock	**R**	coal
	shirt		electricity		paper

Day #1

What is a renewable resource? Give two examples.

A renewable resource is a resource that can be replaced in a person's lifetime. Possible examples: trees, crops, animals

What is an inexhaustible resource? Give two examples.

An inexhaustible resource is a resource that can be used repeatedly and not be used up. Possible examples: sun, air, water

Day #2

Where are most nonrenewable resources found?

Most nonrenewable resources are found under the surface of Earth.

Should nonrenewable resources be used carefully? Explain.

Yes, nonrenewable resources should be used carefully, because once they are used, they are gone and cannot be replaced.

Day #3

What are three ways that people can help conserve natural resources?

Answers will vary.

Day #4

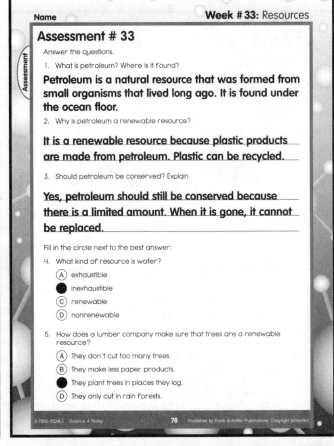

Assessment # 33

Answer the questions.

1. What is petroleum? Where is it found?

Petroleum is a natural resource that was formed from small organisms that lived long ago. It is found under the ocean floor.

2. Why is petroleum a renewable resource?

It is a renewable resource because plastic products are made from petroleum. Plastic can be recycled.

3. Should petroleum be conserved? Explain.

Yes, petroleum should still be conserved because there is a limited amount. When it is gone, it cannot be replaced.

Fill in the circle next to the best answer:

4. What kind of resource is water?
   - (A) exhaustible
   - ● inexhaustible
   - (C) renewable
   - (D) nonrenewable

5. How does a lumber company make sure that trees are a renewable resource?
   - (A) They don't cut too many trees.
   - (B) They make less paper products.
   - ● They plant trees in places they log.
   - (D) They only cut in rain forests.

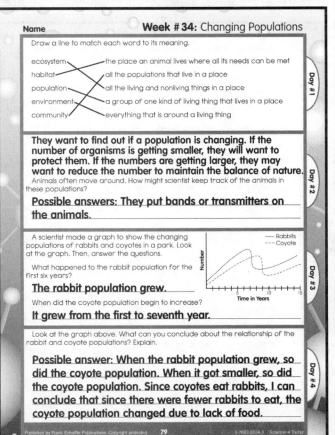

Draw a line to match each word to its meaning.

ecosystem — the place an animal lives where all its needs can be met
habitat — all the populations that live in a place
population — all the living and nonliving things in a place
environment — a group of one kind of living thing that lives in a place
community — everything that is around a living thing

Day #1

They want to find out if a population is changing. If the number of organisms is getting smaller, they will want to protect them. If the numbers are getting larger, they may want to reduce the number to maintain the balance of nature.

Animals often move around. How might scientist keep track of the animals in these populations?

Possible answers: They put bands or transmitters on the animals.

Day #2

A scientist made a graph to show the changing populations of rabbits and coyotes in a park. Look at the graph. Then, answer the questions.

What happened to the rabbit population for the first six years?

The rabbit population grew.

When did the coyote population begin to increase?

It grew from the first to seventh year.

Day #3

Look at the graph above. What can you conclude about the relationship of the rabbit and coyote populations? Explain.

Possible answer: When the rabbit population grew, so did the coyote population. When it got smaller, so did the coyote population. Since coyotes eat rabbits, I can conclude that since there were fewer rabbits to eat, the coyote population changed due to lack of food.

Day #4

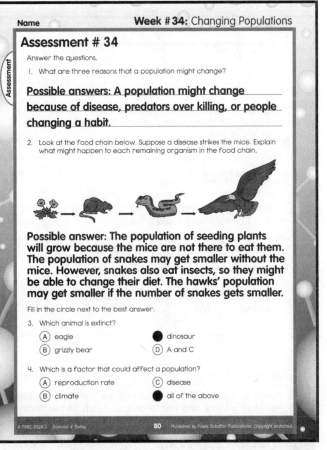

Assessment # 34

Answer the questions.

1. What are three reasons that a population might change?

Possible answers: A population might change because of disease, predators over killing, or people changing a habit.

2. Look at the food chain below. Suppose a disease strikes the mice. Explain what might happen to each remaining organism in the food chain.

Possible answer: The population of seeding plants will grow because the mice are not there to eat them. The population of snakes may get smaller without the mice. However, snakes also eat insects, so they might be able to change their diet. The hawks' population may get smaller if the number of snakes gets smaller.

Fill in the circle next to the best answer.

3. Which animal is extinct?
   - (A) eagle
   - ● dinosaur
   - (B) grizzly bear
   - (D) A and C

4. Which is a factor that could affect a population?
   - (A) reproduction rate
   - (C) disease
   - (B) climate
   - ● all of the above

Answer Key

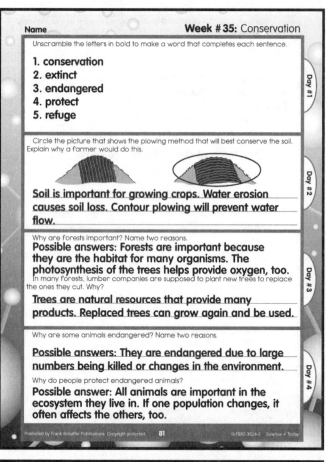

Unscramble the letters in bold to make a word that completes each sentence.

Day #1

1. conservation
2. extinct
3. endangered
4. protect
5. refuge

Day #2

Circle the picture that shows the plowing method that will best conserve the soil. Explain why a farmer would do this.

Soil is important for growing crops. Water erosion causes soil loss. Contour plowing will prevent water flow.

Day #3

Why are forests important? Name two reasons.
Possible answers: Forests are important because they are the habitat for many organisms. The photosynthesis of the trees helps provide oxygen, too.
In many forests, lumber companies are supposed to plant new trees to replace the ones they cut. Why?
Trees are natural resources that provide many products. Replaced trees can grow again and be used.

Day #4

Why are some animals endangered? Name two reasons.
Possible answers: They are endangered due to large numbers being killed or changes in the environment.
Why do people protect endangered animals?
Possible answer: All animals are important in the ecosystem they live in. If one population changes, it often affects the others, too.

Assessment

Assessment # 35

Answer the question.

More than half of all plants and animal species in the world live in the rain forest. Scientists believe that millions more exist, but have not yet been discovered. However, in the last fifty years, nearly half of the rain forests have been destroyed. Why is the rain forest ecosystem important? What are people doing to save it?

Answers will vary.

Day #1

The Romans lived over two thousand years ago. They developed many ideas that we use today. For example, the Romans wanted their rooms to stay warm without having a smoky fire. When building, workers stacked piles of stones on the floor. Then, they built another floor on top, leaving a space between the two. They also built two walls that had spaces between them. Slaves made a huge fire in one of the spaces. The warm air would move through the empty spaces and blew through holes into the rooms.

It is like our central heating. Warm air, made in another place, blows through ducts along ceilings, floors, walls, and into rooms.

Day #2

The Romans built huge cities for people to live in. They needed large amounts of water, but a supply was not available nearby. The Romans designed aqueducts to carry water from a distant water source. They joined arches together, sometimes stacked several stories high, and formed a U-shaped channel on top. The structure was sloped down toward the city so that the water would keep flowing.

How did the Romans use physics to help them get water?
Possible answer: They used the force of gravity to keep water flowing down toward the city.

Day #3

Human waste could have been a problem for so many people living close together. The Romans designed a system to get rid of it. They dug tunnels underground to carry the dirty water and wastes. The Romans built drains in their houses. All sewage was poured down the drain and flowed away.

Why would the Romans want to get rid of sewage?
Possible answer: If the city was not clean, diseases might be a problem.

Day #4

Two thousand years ago, most people used stones or wood to build structures. The Romans wanted to build really big buildings. They couldn't do it with the natural resources they had, so they invented concrete. Concrete was made from small stones, water, and a binding agent, like chalk or volcanic ash. It helped them build huge and very strong structures. The finished texture wasn't pretty, so the Romans decorated the outside with pretty materials.

Possible answer: The different materials could be easily taken to a place and mixed on site, whereas the heavy rock blocks were harder to move and stack.

Assessment

Assessment # 36

Answer the questions.

1. The Romans had great military power. Their huge armies marched all over the land. They took wagons and catapults with them. As a result, they built a huge network of very straight roads. What two problems did the Romans solve with all these the roads?

Possible answers: The armies could move more quickly over land that had roads. They could see where they were going. With straight roads, they could get to places faster, too.

2. Choose one Roman contribution. How does it affect your daily life?

Answers will vary.

Fill in the circle next to the best answer.

3. Which system did the Roman culture borrow from another culture?
   - (A) concrete
   - (B) heating
   - (C) roads
   - ● arches

4. What carries water into houses today?
   - (A) aqueducts
   - ● pipes
   - (C) drains
   - (D) sewers

Answer Key

Name
Week #37: Chinese Contributions

The ancient Chinese drew pictures and wrote about their lives long before anyone else. While learning about the culture is interesting, the material they used to tell the stories is even more interesting—paper! The Chinese invented paper. They first used bamboo sticks tied together. Then, they used silk, which was expensive. Finally, one man experimented with hemp, fishing nets, rags, and bark, which led to a process to make paper.

Day #1

Why was the inventor of paper a good scientist?

Possible answer: He saw a problem, and he worked until he solved it.

The invention of paper led to other discoveries, including ink, wood, or clay tablets to print letters and pictures, and finally the printing press. Before the printing press, only the very rich had books. They hired artists to write books that told the stories and ideas that were important to their culture. The printing press allowed workers to make many copies of the same book cheaply.

Day #2

How could having the technology to print many books change a society?

Possible answer: More people would be able to get books, which meant they could to learn to read and gain more knowledge.

A compass is a device that tells direction. It was very useful to sailors long ago as they traveled on the oceans. It is also a Chinese invention. People rubbed a needle on lodestone, a kind of magnetic rock. When placed in water or tied to a string, it pointed south, which was China's closest magnetic pole.

Day #3

How did the compass affect history?

Possible answer: Because of the compass, people were able to sail long distances, which led to discoveries of new land and people.

Gunpowder is another Chinese invention. One of their early books tells that the Chinese had things called *fire trees* and *silver flowers*, which scientist think were fireworks. Other books tell of how the Chinese used an exploding material on an army who marched into their land.

Day #4

What properties of gunpowder helped the Chinese find a new use for it? Explain.

Gunpowder made fire and loud noises. The fire could hurt people, and the loud noises would scare people who had no knowledge of the material.

Name
Week #37: Chinese Contributions

Assessment # 37

Answer the questions.

1. List ten products made with paper.

Answers will vary.

2. What would your life be like without paper?

Answers will vary.

3. With the exception of paper, which Chinese invention do you think has affected history the most? Explain.

Answers will vary.

Name
Week #38: The History of Flight

Around 1780, Joseph Montgolfier saw smoke rising from a fire. It made him wonder if the smoke could lift something. Montgolfier and his brother held opened paper bags over a fire. They filled with smoke and air, but did not rise very much. Through other experiments, the brothers discovered that it was the hot air that things rise. The discovery led the Montgolfier brothers to build the first hot air balloon. A duck, sheep, and rooster became the first passengers in 1783.

Day #1

What hypothesis might Joseph Montgolfier have made when he saw the smoke rise?

Possible answer: Smoke can make objects fly.

Wilber and Orville Wright enjoyed reading about men who flew gliders. The brothers thought they could make a better flying machine. They began to read books about flying. They experimented with different glider designs and steering devices. Then the Wright brothers added an engine to the glider. In 1903, after many experiments, the Wright brothers flew a machine for 59 seconds.

Day #2

How did experimenting with different designs help the Wright brothers?

Possible answer: They tried different designs to see which worked best. It also gave them ideas on ways to improve the designs.

The helicopter was the first flying machine man thought about. An ancient Chinese toy and drawings by an artist in the late 1400s show such a device. The first helicopter was really built in the 1900s. It tipped over a lot. It wasn't until 1939 that someone made a helicopter that really worked. The inventor made the body smaller and tail longer. He also added a blade to the end of the tail.

Day #3

Possible answer: Yes, failures are important. When scientists fail, they know what doesn't work. They think about how to fix what went wrong. Then, scientists make a new hypothesis and try again.

As early as 1903, scientists were thinking about using rockets to travel up to space. It wasn't until 1957 that the first unmanned space rocket orbited around Earth. In 1961, the first man made a trip around Earth. After that, many people traveled into space. Finally, in 1969, two Americans, Neil Armstrong and Buzz Aldrin, walked on the moon.

Day #4

Why was exploring space important?

Possible answer: Scientists wanted to learn more about the world around them.

Name
Week #38: The History of Flight

Assessment # 38

Complete the page.

1. Use the information from the week to complete a time line to show the history of flight.

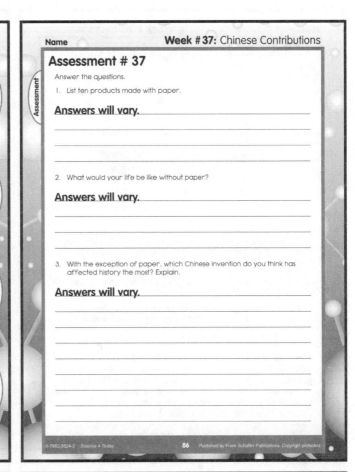

2. How might a scientist use a timeline?

Possible answer: A time line tells a scientist the order and times of events quickly.

3. How does nature affect the development of technology? Give two examples.

Nature often gives scientists ideas for inventions and experiments. Joseph Montgolfier saw the smoke of a fire and thought that it made things rise. The helicopter is based on the way a hummingbird flies and hovers.

Write *true* or *false*.

4. **false** The Montgolfier brothers used smoke to lift the first balloon off the ground.

5. **true** The first passengers to fly were a rooster, duck, and sheep.

6. **false** Gliders were modeled on the Wright brothers' airplane.

7. **true** The first successful helicopter used two blades.

Answer Key

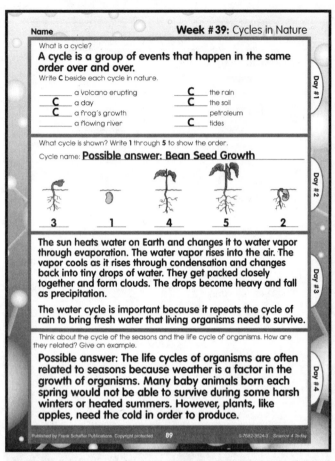

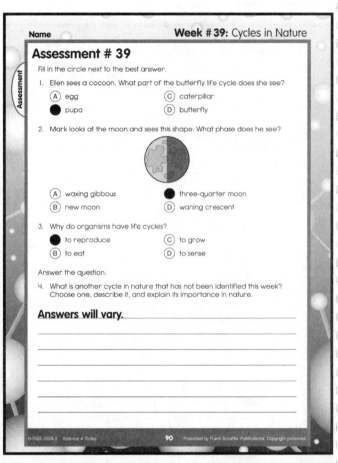

Name

What is a cycle?

A cycle is a group of events that happen in the same order over and over.

Write **C** beside each cycle in nature.

_____ a volcano eruption   **C** the rain
C a day   **C** the soil
C a frog's growth   _____ petroleum
_____ a flowing river   **C** tides

Day #1

What cycle is shown? Write **1** through **5** to show the order.

Cycle name: **Possible answer: Bean Seed Growth**

3   **1**   **4**   **5**   **2**

Day #2

The sun heats water on Earth and changes it to water vapor through evaporation. The water vapor rises into the air. The vapor cools as it rises through condensation and changes back into tiny drops of water. They get packed closely together and form clouds. The drops become heavy and fall as precipitation.

The water cycle is important because it repeats the cycle of rain to bring fresh water that living organisms need to survive.

Day #3

Think about the cycle of the seasons and the life cycle of organisms. How are they related? Give an example.

Possible answer: The life cycles of organisms are often related to seasons because weather is a factor in the growth of organisms. Many baby animals born each spring would not be able to survive during some harsh winters or heated summers. However, plants, like apples, need the cold in order to produce.

Day #4

Name

Assessment

Assessment # 39

Fill in the circle next to the best answer.

1. Ellen sees a cocoon. What part of the butterfly life cycle does she see?
   - (A) egg
   - ● pupa
   - (C) caterpillar
   - (D) butterfly

2. Mark looks at the moon and sees this shape. What phase does he see?

   - (A) waxing gibbous
   - (B) new moon
   - ● three-quarter moon
   - (D) waning crescent

3. Why do organisms have life cycles?
   - ● to reproduce
   - (B) to eat
   - (C) to grow
   - (D) to sense

Answer the question.

4. What is another cycle in nature that has not been identified this week? Choose one, describe it, and explain its importance in nature.

Answers will vary. _____

_____

_____

_____

_____

Name

What is an inventor?

An inventor is a person who first comes up with idea to make something useful.

Name one inventor. Tell what the person invented and tell how it was useful.

Answers will vary. _____

_____

Day #1

Brandon Whale's mother had a pacemaker implanted in her heart. She wore a device on her arm that sent signals through the telephone about her heart to a doctor's office. The device did not fit well, so the signals were not always clear. At the age of eight, Whale came up with a better design so the device fit more like a bracelet. He called it the *PaceMate*. It not only helped his mother, but it helped many other people, too.

Why did Brandon Whale invent the PaceMate?

He saw a problem that needed to be solved to help his mother.

Day #2

Brandon Whale's brother is also an inventor. On visits to the hospital, six-year-old Spencer Whale saw sick children with IVs in their arms trying to ride in toy cars. Parents rolled the IV poles behind the children. Sometimes, the parents tripped over the poles and pulled out the tubes. Spencer Whale decided to attach the IV poles to toy cars. Children could sit inside the cars and ride around the hospital on their own.

What two characteristics made Spencer Whale a good inventor?

Possible answers: He was observant, and he wanted to help.

Day #3

At the age of ten, Taylor Hernandez invented Magic Sponge Blocks. The large building blocks are made of soft sponges. Magnets inside the sponges keep the blocks stacked. When not in use, the blocks can be pressed flat like pancakes for easy storage.

Possible answers: The sponges are light, so if the blocks fall, they will not hurt little children. The blocks can be pressed into a very small size, so they do not take up much space when stored.

Day #4

Name

Assessment

Assessment # 40

Fill in the circle that best answers the question.

1. Why are Magic Sponge Blocks a good invention?
   - (A) They look like pancakes.
   - ● They will not hurt children if they fall.
   - (C) A kid invented them.
   - (D) Magnets are fun toys.

2. Which is a characteristic of a good inventor?
   - ● observant
   - (B) cautious
   - (C) quick
   - (D) selfish

Answer the questions.

3. Is an inventor a scientist? Explain.

Answers will vary. _____

_____

_____

4. Many inventions are made to solve a problem. Think of a problem you would like to solve. Design an invention for it. Explain the invention below and tell how it solves the problem.

Answers will vary. _____

_____

_____

_____
